The

Reference

Shelf

Representative American Speeches 1999-2000

Editors

Calvin M. Logue
Josiah Meigs Professor of Speech
University of Georgia

Lynn Messina, Ph.D.

Jean DeHart
Assistant Professor of Communication Arts
Appalachian State University

The Reference Shelf
Volume 72 • Number 6

The H.W. Wilson Company
2001

The Reference Shelf

The books in this series contain reprints of articles, excerpts from books, addresses on current issues, and studies of social trends in the United States and other countries. There are six separately bound numbers in each volume, all of which are usually published in the same calendar year. Numbers one through five are each devoted to a single subject, providing background information and discussion from various points of view and concluding with a subject index and comprehensive bibliography that lists books, pamphlets, and abstracts of additional articles on the subject. The final number of each volume is a collection of recent speeches, and it contains a cumulative speaker index. Books in the series may be purchased individually or on subscription.

Library of Congress has cataloged this serial title as follows:

Representative American speeches. 1937 / 38–
    New York, H. W. Wilson Co.
        v. 21 cm.—The Reference Shelf
Annual
Indexes:
        Author index: 1937/38–1959/60, with 1959/60;
        1960/61–1969/70, with 1969/70; 1970/71–1979/80,
        with 1979/80; 1980/81–1989/90, 1990.
        Editors: 1937/38–1958/59, A. C. Baird.—1959/60–1969/70, L. Thonssen.—1970/71–
1979/80, W. W. Braden.—1980/81–1994/95, O. Peterson.—1995/96–1998/99 , C. M. Logue
and J. DeHart.—1999/2000– , C. M. Logue, L. Messina, and J. DeHart.
        ISSN 0197-6923 Representative American speeches.
        1. Speeches, addresses, etc., American. 2. Speeches, addresses, etc.
        I. Baird, Albert Craig, 1883–1979 ed. II. Thonssen, Lester, 1904–
        III. Braden, Waldo Warder, 1911–1991 ed.
        IV. Peterson, Owen, 1924– ed. V. Logue, Calvin McLeod, 1935– , Messina, Lynn,
        and DeHart, Jean, eds. VI. Series.
PS668.B3   815.5082   38-27962
                                          MARC-S
Library of Congress [8503r85] rev4

Cover: Donna Shalala, by Liana J. Cooper/Courtesy of the Racine, WI, *Journal Times*

Visit H.W. Wilson's Web site: www.hwwilson.com

Printed in the United States of America

CONTENTS

Preface

The two-year span of 1999–2000 has found America at a unique moment in its history. Simultaneously, its citizens have prepared for the start of a new millennium (complete with fears of a Y2K computer meltdown) and for a changing of the guard, as Bill Clinton's second term in office draws to a close and a presidential election approaches. These two events have prompted the United States to consider more closely where it has been and the direction it should take in the coming century, morally, socially, and politically. This volume contains speeches addressing several issues that are of vital interest to Americans at this time. They represent a wide range of voices—liberal and conservative, majority and minority, male and female, student and professional, private citizen and civil servant. As they express diverse perspectives on a variety of concerns, the speakers included here provide an interesting cross section of views on how Americans perceive themselves, along with their responsibilities to each other and the rest of the world.

The book begins with a section entitled "Looking Backward, Looking Forward," which considers some of the significant moments that have shaped the lives of the American people in the past and regards the future in the context of that history. It begins with the very moving recollections of Sara Martin, a student survivor of the massacre at Columbine High School in April 1999. Next, American Federation of Teachers president Sandra Feldman examines the importance of the labor movement for past and future generations of Americans, while Vice President Al Gore presents his vision for a more accessible "Information Age government" via the Internet. Finally, Deputy Secretary of Defense Rudy de Leon salutes the Tuskegee Airmen in a speech about racial diversity in America's military.

The second section, "Raising the Next Generation," continues the future-oriented tone of Section I by addressing concerns about America's children. James W. Compton, president of the Chicago Urban League, addresses the need for greater personal involvement by communities and parents in the lives of young African-American males. This call for greater adult responsibility in child rearing is echoed by Oklahoma congressman J. C. Watts Jr., though in the context of protecting Americans' right to bear arms. Father Leo J. O'Donovan, president of Georgetown University, then urges adults to turn their attention outward by standing up for causes that directly affect child welfare.

Section III, "Domestic Politics," next considers a few of the so-called "hot-button" issues in American society today—the evolving U.S. trade policy, the changing ethnic population of American voters, and rights for the disabled. U.S. Trade Representative Charlene Barshefsky reviews the effects of the nation's trade policy on Americans during the past century, while Arturo Vargas looks at the largest growing minority population in the country (Latinos) and their potential influence on domestic agenda. Sue Suter, an advocate for the disabled, then addresses the particular concerns of that group by considering the lessons found in the television show *Star Trek: The Next Generation*.

The section which follows, entitled "Health Care," highlights one of the most vigorously debated topics in America today. Floyd D. Loop of the Cleveland Clinic Foundation takes a critical, in-depth look at the effects of government programs like Medicare and other economic factors on the quality of health care in America today. The two speeches which follow offer suggestions for reforming the health care system: Raymond V. Gilmartin, CEO of the pharmaceutical firm Merck, suggests increasing "competition and choice" among providers, while Thomas R. Reardon, the former president of the American Medical Association, asserts that "the physicians of America need to take the lead." Secretary of Health and Human Services Donna E. Shalala then examines health care concerns specific to women, including child care and cancer treatment, and Dr. Ruth Kirchstein of the National Institutes of Health looks at medical issues facing the minority community.

Section V, "Technology and Ethics," explores growing concerns about recent innovations in communications technology and biomedical research, with the speakers in this section discussing both the positive and the more disturbing aspects of these developments. FCC chairman William E. Kennard urges the graduates of Howard University to work towards bridging the gap known as the "digital divide," in which poverty and prejudice deprive people of access to computer technology. U.S. Ambassador to Austria Kathryn Walt Hall then focuses on one of the worst abuses of the World Wide Web, the proliferation of child pornography on the Internet. This address is followed by two others which offer their own takes on the technology revolution currently underway. First, Bill Joy of Sun Microsystems presents an ominous picture of the long-range effects of the latest biotechnological innovations, comparing their cumulative effect to the dropping of an atomic bomb. Professor Glenn McGee of the Center for Bioethics at the University of Pennsylvania takes a less alarmist but equally thoughtful approach in his address on ethical considerations surrounding human cloning, in which he sides with Dr. Ian Wilmut, creator of the cloned sheep Dolly, against any attempt to clone human beings.

The book's final section, as its title reflects, turns to international issues, with speeches that analyze U.S. foreign policy from different points of view. In a speech before the American Enterprise Institute in 1999, the Republican governor Lamar Alexander of Tennessee critiques the Clinton administration's role in international politics, from its actions with NATO, to its attempts at forging a lasting peace in the Middle East, to its diplomatic and economic relations with China. Congressman John J. LaFalce, a Democrat from New York, then offers an opposing perspective, as he expresses his support for trade with China despite that nation's human rights violations. Like Alexander, Kim R. Holmes is critical of President Clinton's foreign policy but focuses on different areas, including the North American Free Trade Agreement (NAFTA), relations with Cuba, and issues of national security. The final speaker, Congressman James P. McGovern of Massachusetts, also addresses U.S. relations with countries south of the border, as he provides a critical and illuminating perspective on the nation's attempts to influence politics in El Salvador.

Special thanks to Gray Young, Denise M. Bonilla, Jacquelene Latif, and Sara Yoo for their assistance on this book.

I. Looking Backward, Looking Forward

Commencement Speech for Columbine High School, 1999[1]

Sara Martin

Undergraduate student, St. John's College, Annapolis, MD; born Aurora, CO, 1982; graduate of Columbine High School, CO, with a 3.8 GPA

Editors' introduction: Sara Martin addressed fellow high school graduates and students, parents, faculty, friends, and members of the community at Columbine High School commencement. One month earlier, on April 20, two students from her school killed 12 (including one teacher) and wounded 22 of her fellow classmates. In the speech below, Ms. Martin explained how "we are created by the choices we make." The tragedy taught that "I must live life with a concentrated purpose and a dedication to each moment." The speech was broadcast over CNN and on ABC and CBS outlets in Colorado. Later Ms. Martin was asked to be interviewed for CBS's "Most Fascinating Women of the Year," in conjunction with the *Ladies Home Journal*.

Sara Martin's speech: During World War II, with threats of disastrous bombings the people of Cambridge England set out to preserve the exquisite stain glass windows of Kings College Chapel. The people rallied together and took apart the windows and numbered each piece. Then, families took the fragments and hid them within their homes. They tucked them away in sugar bowls and sock drawers.

The chapel made it through the war unharmed and the people brought back the pieces and reconstructed the windows according to their numbers. Though rebuilt, visible still between the replaced fragments of the window are the lines where the pieces were broken, and then put back together. Maybe the beauty now revealed in the light is that an entire community came together and restored the vision. Though flawed, I believe it was made stronger than ever.

In a way, each and every one of us is piece of a Columbine community stain glass through which the sun shines bright and against which the wind blows cold. The piece we carry into our

---

1. Delivered in Littleton, Colorado, on May 22, 1999, at 10:30 a.m. Reprinted with permission of Sara Martin.

homes is made up of elements given to us by the literature that we read, the great teachers we learn from, and the models we observe. It is a vision within us of which the totality is unknown until we die.

And in some ways our piece of the greater window is a stained window in itself made up of pieces from our own experiences. Our window is not unlike the window of the Annunciation within the chapel. It is made of pieces of glass given to us like messages to a child. It is our responsibility to accept those pieces. If we cherish them, we begin to create the pictures of our own window and determine the colors and their hue.

For me, the *Iliad* combined with the *Odyssey,* as an examination of human civilization is painted in a rich medieval blue, somewhere on my own window. Alongside it, decorated in deep, fragrant yellows

---

In a way, each and every one of us is piece of a Columbine community stain glass through which the sun shines bright and against which the wind blows cold.

---

and greens are John Steinbeck's great works of literature: *Of Mice and Men* and *Cannery Row*—stories of simple human beings achieving great acts of love.

For all of us here, our teachers are often the greatest givers of the glass. For example, Mr. Sneddon and his vision for his students that extends beyond the curriculum of Earth Science but encompasses life lessons: skills he considers valuable that I now consider priceless.

These are gifts if you open your heart.

There's also Mrs. Sampson who met a ram at the stock show with spiritual eyes and who sees books as a thicket that one must subdue. I've never been a poet, but with her, I've learned to live the poetry. There's Mr. Tonelli and his overflowing love for every student who walks into his classroon. There's Mr. Andres, Sr. and Jr., who have brought dedication to a Columbine tradition of music and have provided me with a personal melody for my past four years. And Mrs. Jankowski and the quilts we made in journalism just so she'd have a square of cloth to remember us by.

These are pieces that make up my window that adds to the overall window of our Columbine community.

The models in life, my mom as a teacher and Paula Reed as a coach and an encourager, have added greatly to the colors that enhance my glass. I watch these women who bring grace and beauty to motherhood and I take those pieces and I hold onto them.

It is our job to hear the message and to recognize the pieces. We are created by the choices we make. Our own window can be vibrant in color and spirit—a collection of the gifts given to us by the people who surround us. Or, our window can be blurred and colorless. We must recognize the pieces. Hear the message and create the window within us.

Because of what occurred on April 20, I am beginning to see what my personal window must reflect in order to fit into the larger window. I must live life with a concentrated purpose and a dedication to each moment. I must remember our friends who lost their lives——especially my friend Cassie Bernall. And as I wish that I had had more time, and more opportunities to tell her what she meant to me, I must recognize what I have learned: to love deeply and to appreciate every word and every gesture of every person I love or will love.

So, now, we are being called upon particularly at this time, to restore the vision—to take our numbered pieces and rebuild the window of our community. And though we have faced disasters of our own and our window may appear to have been shattered, we can achieve a greater beauty as we put the pieces back together again

Let the light shine through the stained glass, colored by these last four years, these last four weeks. Like the people of Cambridge, let us recognize what is worthy to be saved, to be restored, and in unity rebuild the Columbine window from which others may draw their inspiration.

The Labor Movement[2]

Our Children's Future

Sandra Feldman

President, American Federation of Teachers, 1997– ; born in New York City; B.A., Brooklyn College; M.A., English, New York University; teacher and United Federation of Teachers (UFT) chapter leader at PS 34, Manhattan; field representative, UFT, 1966–83; executive director, UFT 1983–86; secretary, UFT, 1983–86; president, UFT, New York City, and vice president, AFT, 1986–97; Executive Council of the AFL-CIO, 1997– ; Council on Competitiveness; co-chair, Child Labor Coalition; National Board for Professional Teaching Standards; chair, AFL-CIO Committee on Social Policy; selected one of New York City's "75 Most Influential Women" by Crain's New York Business and one of the "100 Most Influential Women in America" by Ladies Home Journal.

Editors' introduction: In the Annual Distinguished Labor Leader Address to the Chicago-Kent College of Law, President Sandra Feldman cautioned some 300 labor leaders to realize that, even with a strong economy, "our prosperity is less widely shared than at any time since the Roaring Twenties." "Unions," she insisted, "can offer professionals the collegial contact and collective clout that they need."

Sandra Feldman's speech: The Chicago Federation of Labor and Chicago-Kent College of Law deserve a great deal of credit for founding the Institute for Law and the Workplace. The Institute performs an important service by bringing people together from labor, management, and the legal profession to discuss issues facing our workplaces and our world. And I especially appreciate your efforts to help young people learn more about the part that organized labor plays in the American community.

Today, you have asked me to talk about "The Labor Movement and our Children's Future." And I'm especially interested in talking to those of you who are our future—those of you who are preparing to begin your careers.

You aren't children any longer—but many of you went to good public schools because labor fought to establish them at the end of the 19th century. Many of you were inoculated against diseases because labor fought for health programs that made it possible; and

---

2. Delivered in Chicago, Illinois, March 2, 2000, at noon. Reprinted with permission of Sandra Feldman.

none of you had to work in the awful conditions that children found themselves in before labor won the passage of child labor law—a fight we're still making for children around the world.

In the year 2000, most children in America have a better future because of fights that unions made.

So my message to you today is that the future of America's children is tied to the future of labor's fight for working families; and even if you think you're never going to work in a place or a profession where unions are active, you should still want an America with a strong and vibrant labor movement.

And, because the ultra-competitive new economy has a way of turning even the most skilled jobs into temporary positions and even the most highly educated people into disposable parts, you may need a union yourself one day.

But, while unions deserve your support, we also need to earn it. We need to reach out to the new American workforce, including professionals and technical employees. We need to give them voice and be a vehicle for enabling them to accomplish their best work. And we need to help people find their way in a new economy where permanent jobs are becoming a thing of the past, large institutions are changing or crumbling, and security depends on constantly learning new skills.

The real lesson of the past half century is: "What's good for working Americans and their unions is also good for America."

Back in the 1950s, when the big three auto-makers dominated the American economy, the president of the biggest company of all, a fellow nicknamed "Engine Charlie" Wilson, declared—and I repeat a well-worn quote: "What's good for General Motors is good for America."

The real lesson of the past half century is: "What's good for working Americans and their unions is also good for America."

From the end of World War II through the early seventies, America prospered.

And that era of shared prosperity was also the high-water mark for American unions. Union membership reached its highest point in 1954: 35%. During that period, unions were able to win rising wages and better benefits not only for their own members but for unrepresented workers as well. We created a huge middle class during those years. And we invented things that Americans now take for granted—like weekends.

After 1973, recession hit, layoffs and downsizing occurred, and union membership declined. And so did the standard of living for working Americans. From 1973 through 1995, workers' real

wages—what people's paychecks can actually buy—declined by
11%. And one important reason was that union strength had
declined.

For the past five years—thanks largely to the Clinton/Gore
administration's policies—our economy is as prosperous as it's ever
been, and real wages are finally increasing again. But—largely
because unions still represent a relatively small share of the workforce—our prosperity is less widely shared than at any time since
the Roaring Twenties.

The well-being of America and the success of the labor movement
are interdependent. That's because unions not only help people
raise their living standards, they help people raise their voices, in
their workplaces—and in the larger society, as well. Unions give
voice to the needs and desires of working families for healthcare, for
the education of their children, for economic justice and a fair share
of the American dream. That's why they are essential institutions in
any free society—and why dictatorships do all they can to shut
them down.

Unions lift living standards, encourage equality, and strengthen
democracy by helping people win a voice in the decisions that shape
their jobs and their lives.

In the civil rights movement unsung heroes were often African-
American trade unionists like A. Philip Randolph. In South Africa,
the black coal miners union provided the shock troops in the struggle against apartheid. And in eastern Europe in the 1980's, the
death blow to Communism was dealt by Solidamosc, a movement of
trade unions.

And the American labor movement assisted in every one of those
struggles.

So, when employers resort to intimidation and even illegal firings
of workers who are trying to organize, they are threatening the fabric of democracy, in my opinion.

Yet, in America, about 10,000 workers lose their jobs every year
for supporting union organizing campaigns where they work.

Half of all employers threaten to eliminate workers' jobs if they
join together in a union. Four-fifths train their supervisors to
frighten workers out of supporting the union. And nine out of ten
hold mandatory, closed-door meetings with workers to make sure
they understand that the company does not want them to join the
union.

This intimidation and indoctrination explains why only about 10%
of the workers in the private sector are represented by unions. In
the public sector, employers are less likely to bend or break the law

to prevent their employees from organizing. And that is why more than 35% of public employees in this country have chosen to join unions.

But not all public employers practice fairness, even though the law requires it. Right here in Chicago, for example, and on the Champaign campus, the venerable University of Illinois is fighting against the unionization of graduate employees. Graduates have been denied the right to a recognition election, even though they teach nearly half of all undergraduate classes, do critical research, and hold office hours. These are *jobs*; the employees pay taxes, they can be fired—and their fight for a union is far from over.

It is a sad fact that, with honorable exceptions, American management is more hostile to unions than their counterparts in any other advanced democracy in the world.

But today's unions are devoting more energy, more imagination, and more resources to helping workers organize unions. And these efforts are beginning to bear fruit.

Last year, at least 600,000 workers organized or joined unions. That was an increase of more than 25% over 1998. (The AFT had a particularly good year—better than most.)

But a closer look reveals how much harder unions have to work and how much faster we have to grow if we are going to become a force for change for working Americans in every industry and occupation.

Because of layoffs and other job losses even in these prosperous times, the net increase in union membership was 265,000. Even that was the largest net annual increase in 20 years. But, because we were growing no faster than the economy, the percentage of workers who belong to unions just held steady at 13.9%.

So we reversed decades of decline. And that's good—but not good enough.

To grow further and faster, we have to do a better job of organizing the fastest-growing sectors of the American workforce.

One dirty little secret of the new economy is that some of the fastest-growing jobs—such as home-care workers, nursing home workers, food service workers to name just a few—pay low wages, provide few benefits, and offer little opportunity for upward mobility. They also make it difficult for children in these families—imagine parents having to choose between paying for a class trip or an inhaler for an asthmatic child, let alone having the resources to buy a home computer.

Unions are performing a real service by helping these workers to organize. In the AFT, we represent more than 175,000 school support staff, including food service workers, bus drivers, and classroom aides.

When I started out as a teacher in New York City during the 1960s, teacher aides worked for the minimum wage, with no benefits and no reason to believe that their future held anything better.

But our union put the teachers' clout in their corner. We helped paraprofessionals organize, bargain better wages, and obtain their first health and pension benefits. We built a career ladder, and many now can complete college and become teachers.

Unionization certainly does work for low-wage workers.

But the other dirty little secret of the new economy is that among the fastest growing jobs are professional, technical, and knowledge workers who have few benefits and little security. In fact, these employees are already the third largest sector of the workforce. And they are expected to account for one-fourth of all new jobs that are being created between 1996 and 2006.

These professional workers have economic concerns, as other workers do. And as the strike by engineers at Boeing has demonstrated, a growing number of professionals are ready, willing, and able to act on these concerns.

But just as strongly, they want to uphold the standards of their profession. They want a stronger voice in decisions, and they are passionately committed to improving the quality of the services they provide.

As individuals, they have very little power to do this.

But, unions can offer professionals the collegial contact and collective clout that they need.

At the American Federation of Teachers, we've grown to more than a million members by organizing professionals who experts said would never join unions—public school teachers, college and university professors, nurses and health professionals, and skilled employees in state and local governments.

Over the past few years, we've organized or affiliated more than 37,000 teachers and education professionals in Puerto Rico; more than 9,500 teachers, librarians, and counselors in Dallas; 17 units of nurses and health care professionals in New Jersey and Pennsylvania; and more than 3,300 psychologists in New York State—and I'll say more about them a little later.

Our union has grown by giving voice to professionals' concerns with improving education, health care, and other services they provide.

Over my many years with the AFT—from classroom teacher, to local leader and national president—I don't know how many times I've carried picket signs with the slogan, "Teachers want what children need."

Other professional constituencies have the same kinds of concerns. Of all the nurses with whom I've worked, I've met many more who want to take on hospital administrators over better staffing levels than want to hit the bricks for better salaries. And social workers are just as dedicated to reducing caseload sizes, so that they can treat their clients as people, not paperwork.

To achieve these improvements, unions need to be strong, imaginative, and flexible.

Here in Chicago, where the AFT was founded, the Teachers Union enjoys so much support from its members that, even after the Legislature eliminated collective bargaining in this city, the teachers maintained their union—and their contract.

With this strength, the union has been able to work with the Mayor and the Superintendent of Schools on comprehensive and collaborative reforms to improve the education of Chicago's children, including re-designing low performing schools.

In addition, the CTU has created a visionary new institution—the QuEST Center—which helps provide teachers and support staff with the professional tools they need to do their jobs better.

In this fluid economy, unions must also be a source of economic security for workers.

The CTU's efforts show how unions can promote quality and institutional change. The union couldn't be a force for change if it weren't strong. And it couldn't stay strong without being a force for change.

In this fluid economy, unions must also be a source of economic security for workers. Even the most highly skilled workers have to move from job to job and employer to employer. Just as the Building Trades Unions have always done, unions for professionals need to provide the services that knowledge workers need to stabilize their lives—training and retraining, health coverage, retirement security, and representation on issues of concern to the industry as a whole.

In higher education, we can see how even the most highly educated workers have had to become economic nomads. The AFT is helping the folks who have come to be called "Roads Scholars"—and "road" is spelled "R.O.A.D."—instructors who have to keep moving from position to position and from college to college.

From 1970 to 1997, the percentage of professors who work part-time nearly doubled from 22% to 42.5%. The biggest explosion has been at two-year colleges, where part-timers now comprise fully 69% of new hires. These part-time faculty now represent about a third of the more than 100,000 college faculty represented by the AFT.

This raises issues of exploitation and education. When part-time faculty often earn little more than $1,500 a course, when most receive little or no health or retirement benefits, and when they aren't paid for office hours advising students—we have to wonder how long our colleges can keep attracting the best instructors.

Yes, most part-time faculty do good jobs under trying conditions. But the students deserve professors whose minds are on the subjects they're teaching, not how they're going to pay the rent.

That is why our higher-education affiliates here in Illinois are working to organize part-time faculty, to win higher salaries, job protections and due process, and to give them a leg up when permanent jobs become available.

These "Roads Scholars" are one face of the new economy. The psychologists who just joined AFT are another.

Just like a growing number of workers, the psychologists are self-employed entrepreneurs. They don't expect to work under a union contract.

But, just like many other professionals, they find that the ultra-competitive new economy is doing violence to their values. Their patients—many suffering from debilitating illnesses—depend on their therapist's professional expertise to help them recover.

Now, managed-care companies have come between the professional and the patient. If administrators say that someone with a particular condition is eligible for only five visits, their word is law—even though they have never seen the patient and have no way of judging the patient's particular needs.

Of course, this is a bread-and-butter issue. But most psychologists are far more concerned about the overriding of their professional judgement, and they are outraged about the harm it can do to some of their patients. And they joined our union to strengthen their voices and raise them on behalf of their patients' needs.

It's a long way from the construction workers and coal miners who founded the labor movement at the end of the 19th century to the professors and psychologists who are joining our ranks at the beginning of the 21st.

But, in many ways, they are seeking the same things. They want to be more than economic nomads. They want to work together with others in their occupations to make their jobs better. And they want the opportunity to do their best work for the people they serve and be respected and fairly paid for it.

It is up to our unions to find new ways to help them organize their workplaces, address their needs, and advance their values. If we fail, our movement will dwindle and die.

But, if we succeed, you and all of America will benefit from the existence of a movement that fights for a shared prosperity and a stronger democracy. A movement that will stand ready, if you need us, to help you win more security in your livelihoods and more dignity in your lives.

That is why the young people who are our future should want a strong labor movement in America—and that is why we are working harder than ever to make sure you will have one.

Thank you.

E-government for the 21st Century[3]

Al Gore

Vice President of the United States, 1993– , and Democratic candidate for president of the United States, 2000; born in Washington, D.C., March 31, 1948; raised in Carthage, TN, and Washington, D.C.; B.A., government, Harvard University, 1969; U.S. Army in Vietnam 1969–71; reporter, the Tennessean, *1971–76; Vanderbilt University Divinity School and Vanderbilt Law School 1974–76; representative from Tennessee, U.S. House of Representatives, 1977–85; U.S. senator (D) from Tennessee, 1984–93; author* Earth in the Balance: Ecology and the Human Spirit, *1992.*

Editors' introduction: Vice President Al Gore spoke in an indoor atrium to some 150 persons on the North Carolina State University Centennial Campus of Raleigh/Durham. In a presidential campaign speech, Vice President Gore envisioned a "form of government" that was more responsive, one in which "services are on-line and interactive." He suggested that in this virtual structure, "the cost of government will go down."

Al Gore's speech: It's great to be here in the fabled Research Triangle, to talk about America's future. It's great to be here at North Carolina State's Centennial Campus—in the middle of what is rightly called the campus of the future.

I'm here to invite you and the American people to join me in making a national commitment to create a more responsive form of government—we might think of it as "e-government"—in which the best of government services are on-line and interactive, so the people have their government at their fingertips—and so they can help create solutions themselves and better take charge of their own communities and lives.

Today, I'm releasing a comprehensive plan for the kind of Information Age government I want to create.

With your help, as President, I will lead a second American revolution—to make our self-government far less costly, far more effective, and far more relevant to every American.

Americans are the experts on the problems and solutions in their own communities. The Internet should be put to the service of community and citizen empowerment in a whole new way—so every citizen, whether in the Research Triangle or a small town square, can

---

3. Delivered in Raleigh/Durham, North Carolina, on June 5, 2000, at 3:00 p.m.

instantly tap new skills, new tools, access to information about everything from health care to education, and even access to capital to start or ramp up your own business. The government on-line should help you remove barriers to opportunity, and find new knowledge to help you take on a disability. The power of government should not be locked away in Washington, but put at your service—no further away than your keyboard.

People don't care at all what department or agency or office has specific jurisdiction over the information or tools or resources that you need. And you shouldn't have to care. You shouldn't have to fill out endless forms, or worry about somebody who's having a bad day giving you the runaround. You shouldn't have to wait in line to communicate with your self-government. Taxpayers shouldn't have to expect that every week will bring more examples of obvious waste and inefficiency. You should be able to have a sense of confidence and high expectation in the years ahead as you relate to a new system of e-government.

With your help, I will tear down all the barriers between the different departments and agencies of our government, and obliterate the barriers between you and the clear, understandable, responsive common sense that you have a right to expect.

Imagine being able to call up in the blink of an eye a list of every health plan in your area—to judge for yourself which offered the best quality of care. You could speak to a specialist, halfway across the country—to talk about your treatment, discover the latest medical advances that concerned you or a loved one, or get the best advice on your medication.

Imagine when community policing gets the help of ordinary citizens committed to law and order in their neighborhoods and willing to join together to keep the peace. Every citizen and police department could share resources, logging onto an interactive map of crime trends in every neighborhood. And the citizens would help shape the database because they are the real experts in the lives of their communities: a homebound grandmother could send an officer an instant e-mail to report dangerous behavior on a street corner, or community members could give leads about crimes to their neighborhood police.

Imagine if a child in the poorest neighborhood could have access to the richest educational materials and most illustrious museums; could turn on a computer at her desk at school, and click her way through the National Gallery—from the stunning landscapes of Georgia O'Keefe, to the majestic portraits of Frederick Remington, to the richly complex works of Jackson Pollack.

And imagine what those breakthroughs, and others yet to be invented by American creativity and curiosity, could do for an electorate that is too often alienated, and often feels voiceless in a system corroded by special interests and powerless to make change.

Imagine how such electronic forms of citizen empowerment could help restore our faith in self-government—our trust in a true American community, where we can all share in the greatest gifts of our time and have a direct say in how we govern ourselves.

Imagine how the cost of government will go down, and how our pride in the way our democracy works will go up. You have seen in the last few years what this revolution can mean in the way you relate over the Internet to businesses that didn't exist before you started surfing the Web. You know what I'm talking about when I describe this vision of e-government.

I know we can do this together. I know how we can do this together. And I know that every single tool that we need to make this vision a reality already exists. The only piece that remains to be put in place is the mandate that I am asking you for today.

This is about something far greater than government services, or government streamlining. It is the heart of what we must do to revitalize the ideal that has animated our democracy since its founding––that the people are the master and government is the servant.

We have to make that ideal real in each new generation. In the words of Thomas Jefferson, "our laws and institutions must move forward hand-in-hand with the progress of the human mind."

The United States has proven the principle that the average citizen is the best decision-maker.

Early in our history, if you had a question about your taxes, or your retirement benefits, you could visit a government office in person. In fact, that was often the only choice you had.

That's why, in President Lincoln's day, our government opened agricultural field offices within a single day's horseback ride of every farmer in America.

And by the way—we ended that policy in this administration, over 130 years later.

I must say, it's a wonderful illustration of bureaucracy—a policy designed to help people with horses outlasted the coming of the railroad and the invention of the automobile.

After the Civil War, veterans who wanted to get their pensions had to come all the way to Washington, DC, to personally visit the pension office. There is still a massive, high-ceilinged lobby in that building—designed so veterans could leave their horses there when they applied for their pensions. That was the 19th Century's idea of customer service.

In fact, let me tell you a little more about it. If you were a veteran, you had to wait around for a clerk to look through all the Civil War records, until your papers were found. The papers were bound with red tape—which was cut to see if you were in fact eligible for a pension. And so a whole generation of Americans learned about "cutting red tape."

This generation can do that with e-government. By putting public services on-line, we will make dramatic savings—eliminating not only the red tape, but most of the paper that used to be wrapped in the tape.

I will set clear goals, and I tell you today that we will measure the performance of e-government regularly and rigorously. I will put progress reports on line, so every American can see what we've been able to achieve—and where we've fallen short. And the reports will be interactive, so people can e-mail their own ideas, tell us about the special challenges in their own communities, and help us shape solutions. In this way, we can make e-government a true Information Age town square—which can be a unique, 21st Century contribution to the vision and the reality of self-government.

E-government will be accessible, and easy for families to use. We will protect the privacy of all Americans—because the right to privacy is a fundamental right, which calls for special safeguards in the Information Age. We have to make all e-government a model of good conduct and the right values on the Internet. For example, we will make sure people with disabilities can log on and get any special help they need in a way they can use it. And we have to make sure the American people have their complaints heard and answered—quickly and fully.

I'll push for tens of billions of dollars in savings by making all major government purchases on the Internet. We'll create a new on-line auction site—we'll call it "g-bay"—to sell off equipment the government no longer needs. And then we'll invest the savings in even greater efficiency, more innovation, and better services for our people.

If I'm entrusted with the Presidency, together we can use this technology to ensure that by 2004, we can look back on the time before e-government, and it will seem as outdated and antiquated as government before the telephone seems today.

There is no longer any reason for any of us to accept a one-size-fits-all approach in the public sector. Together, we will transform America's collection of ramshackle bureaucracies into an e-government that works for you—each and every one of you.

In doing so, we will seize upon the explosive potential of the Internet across our entire society.

When the first computer was invented 55 years ago, it took up 15,000 square feet. When the head of IBM saw it for the first time, he asked why it was so hot in the room. It was because that computer needed 18,000 radio tubes just to keep running.

Today, there is more computer power in a small pocket calculator that costs about ten dollars. And generates a lot less heat.

A few years ago, I was talking with a group of college students about the amazing pace of technology. And I pointed out that if today's cars made the same advances as computers, a Cadillac would get 100,000 miles to the gallon—and cost about 50 cents.

Then one of the students in the front row said: "Sure, but it would be about this big."

Well, today's breakthrough products may not always be big—but tomorrow's horizons are limitless.

In 1992, only a small number of physicists were using the World Wide Web. There were only 50 web sites. Today, there are 300 million people connected to the Web on every part of the globe.

So far, only a third of all manufacturers do business on-line—and e-commerce accounts for less than one percent of all sales.

But a new report today from the Commerce Department that I released this morning shows that even at that level, the impact on our economy is already enormous.

Information technology has contributed almost a third of all our economic growth in the past five years. It is enabling small start-ups to compete with large corporations, across all industries. It has led to higher wages for American families, and higher incomes at all income levels; and it has generated as much as half of all our productivity growth in recent years.

Our challenge now is to make this technology work for all of our people.

Black or white, rich or poor, a Ph.D. or a self-taught genius, the Internet reflects back your guts and your gifts, not your complexion or gender. A CEO or a self-taught cyber-surfer, a busy housewife with a vision and a marketing plan, or a group of guys working after hours in someone's garage—whoever you are, the Internet doesn't care so long as you have a good idea. This has helped turn our best values into reality by helping to open the gates to a more level playing field.

We need a national commitment to move America ahead and keep America at the forefront of the new economy—to create more jobs and more high-paying jobs. I believe we should double America's investment in information technology—and make sure the Internet remains a global free trading zone.

We must finish the job of connecting every classroom and library in America to the Internet. From the poorest inner-city school district to the finest magnet school—every child should have access to the same vast store of knowledge and discovery.

America was the pioneer of universal education; now let's set a goal for the first decade of the 21st Century: let's make America the first nation on Earth with universal computer literacy. We'll post that goal on the Internet, and ask every part of government and every level of government—from our Education Department and the National Science Foundation to local school boards—to help us meet it. We'll involve our universities and the private sector. The emphasis will be on results, not red tape.

We must also launch a new crusade—again calling on both public and private resources—to move toward full Internet access in every home, for every family, all across the United States. The next Thomas Edison or Marie Curie may be a child waiting in a ghetto or a rural hollow for the tools to learn and experiment; let's get him—or her—wired and on-line. We must not rest until Internet access is as common as telephone access in every American household.

And then we must put the most effective, the most responsive, the most interactive e-government we can create on every desktop in America—so that every home, every office, and every classroom are truly wired for democracy. We can harness the newest technology to advance our oldest and most fundamental goals and values.

Imagination, properly focused, has always been the inexhaustible spiritual energy which we have applied to the productive work we are intended to do on this Earth as Americans. In this way, America has given the world great gifts.

If I'm entrusted with the Presidency, I will work for a government that strives to be as good as our best technology—and as good as the American people.

I will work for an e-government that uses the Internet and the information technology to make real improvements and real empowerment to all our people.

And I will bring government closer to our people—just a couple of clicks away from every citizen, everywhere in this nation.

You are on the front lines of the revolution in technology. Let's use it to restore trust in government's most basic mission: to help, to serve, to listen, and to respond to the American people. Thank you.

Address to Tuskegee Airmen, Inc. 29th National Convention[4]

Rudy de Leon

Deputy Secretary of Defense, 1997– ; B.A., history, Loyola University, Los Angeles, 1974; graduate executive program, Harvard University, 1984; Seminar XXI, foreign politics, Massachusetts Institute of Technology, 1987; legislative assistant, U.S. Senate and U.S. House of Representatives, 1975–85; staff director, Committee on Armed Services, U.S. House of Representatives, 1989–93; special assistant to the Secretary of defense, 1993–94; Under Secretary, U.S. Air Force, 1994–97; Under Secretary of Defense for Personnel and Readiness, 1997–2000; has received several awards and honors for public service.

Editors' Introduction: At a luncheon in August 2000, Deputy Secretary of Defense Rudy de Leon spoke to an audience of active and retired members of the U.S. military gathered at Lackland Air Force Base in San Antonio, Texas. Among them were the World War II pilots known as the Tuskegee Airmen, members of an African-American squadron who trained at Tuskegee, Alabama. In the speech he praises the pilots' heroism during the war and lauds their current efforts to "teach another generation of Americans about the high price of freedom, and about the importance of fairness and dignity and opportunity"—lessons that he says many in America's private sector still need to learn.

Rudy de Leon's speech: Thank you, General [Lester] Lyles [Commander, Air Force Materiel Command], for the introduction. It's a great opportunity to be here today and to participate with this group. Lieutenant Colonel Clark Kent [Squadron Commander, Randolph Air Force Base], I asked him, is that his real name. He said it's his Air Force handle. [Laughter] He introduced some of the very senior people here at the head table. But I also see that our Reserve and Guard leaders, not only from the Pentagon but from other installations around the corner, around the country—in General [Daniel] James' [III] case, it is around the corner—are here, but I would ask all of our military people who are in attendance to just stand for one second. [Applause]

Forty years ago, President Kennedy challenged us to ask not what our country could do for us, but what we could do for our country. The men and women in uniform who just stood are the embodiment

---

4. Delivered on August 11, 2000, at Lackland Air Force Base, San Antonio, Texas.

of that commitment. Indeed, we are proud of their service, whether they are here with us in San Antonio this afternoon or in Korea or Kosovo or Bosnia or Saudi Arabia.

Additionally, with so many luminaries here and so many senior general officers, I would like to briefly just introduce the [Tuskegee Airmen's] Military Affairs Luncheon Committee and ask them to stand, because they've put in a lot of work here today, too. Lieutenant Colonel Joseph Ward; Colonel Doc War; Lieutenant Colonel William Clark Kent; Major Derek Green; and Major Cheryl Malone. [Applause] Logistics are important and organization. So thank you very much.

Thank you for inviting me to speak to you today. It's truly an honor to share a dais with a group of men and women who have done so much not only for the security of America and the protection of its interests abroad, but for progress and social justice here at home.

Together the Tuskegee Airmen and the Organization of Black Airline Pilots have much to be proud of, and it's wonderful to come here and be reminded of how much you've accomplished in schools, in communities, and for the young men and women who serve in uniform, and to see how much energy and enthusiasm you are bringing to your new endeavors.

So for that, I want to thank you for the honor of appearing before a group, the Tuskegee Airmen, that in the 20th Century—which has been a century of aviation, of the exploration of space—the Tuskegee Airmen rightfully stand high on that list of accomplishment.

The New York Times on page five, 4th of July, 1943, ran this article. Dateline, Allied Headquarters, in North Africa. Quote, "An American Negro fighter squadron escorting bombers yesterday over Sicily destroyed a Focke-Wulfe 190 to score the formation's first victory. General Dwight D. Eisenhower was on the airfield to congratulate First Lieutenant Charles Hall of Brazil, Indiana, when he returned after shooting down the plane. The Commander in Chief also congratulated Lieutenant Colonel Benjamin O. Davis, Jr., of Washington, D.C., squadron commander, on the unit's first victory."

The article goes on to give Lieutenant Hall's description of the encounter, and in the very last paragraph it stated that he attended the Illinois State Teachers College for three years, but left there to begin his flight training in 1941, and it gave his age— 21 years old.

I cannot help but think what a proud and triumphant day that must have been for all the Tuskegee Airmen, for so many of you who had trained so long and so hard, to have defied the odds and the predictions of the critics and the cynics, and to have persisted despite an oppressive climate. There was the proof in *The New York Times*, complete with a handshake from General Eisenhower. A young African American, a Tuskegee Airman, scored a victory at the age of 21 that most men could never accomplish in their entire lives. And America learned about it appropriately, on the 4th of July. [Applause]

That qualifies as a great milestone for all Americans because it is one of those simple occasions when an undeniable fact puts to lie the myths and the irrational fears that fueled America's racism.

I believe that is why those of you here have had such a powerful and positive effect on our country. You said, "We have the talent. Just give us one chance, and we will show you a truth so strong about our character, about our courage, about our commitment to our nation that it can never be denied." Then you demonstrated that truth. You held it up for all Americans, and it was a truth so powerful that it still echoes today.

> *A young African American, a Tuskegee Airman, scored a victory at the age of 21 that most men could never accomplish in their entire lives.*

As you know, two years ago the United States made right a wrong and awarded General [Benjamin O.] Davis his fourth star . . . [Applause] . . . which was so long in coming, but was so well deserved. President Clinton said at his presentation—and Colonel [Charles] McGee [retired, President of the Tuskegee Airmen, Inc.] was one of the people to speak in the program that afternoon at the White House—President Clinton said in his presentation, "When the doors were shut on him, he knocked again and again until finally they opened. Until his sheer excellence and determination made it impossible to keep them closed. And once the doors were open, he made sure that they stayed open for others to follow."

Then Secretary [of Defense, William S.] Cohen said, "Few did more than General Davis to prove that black and white Americans could not only serve together, indeed that white soldiers could serve under a black superior, but that they could succeed together."

I believe that the same could be said of every one of the Tuskegee Airmen. Each of you in your own way has kept the doors open for others to follow. Every year by sharing your history and giving your time and talent you teach another generation of Americans about the high price of freedom, and about the importance of fairness and dignity and opportunity. And your work continues, whether it be through scholarships, grants, mentoring programs, or countless other ways that you are touching the lives of young people throughout the country.

The examples of your dedication and perseverance made a difference half a century ago in places ranging from Tuskegee, Alabama, to Selfridge, Michigan to North Africa to Italy, and it continues to make a difference today in ways that few could have imagined when they read that article on July 4, 1943. While we are familiar with the history and all that has been written about your exploits and struggles here in America and over North Africa and Europe, I found out something very interesting the other day. If you were to go to the cutting edge of information technology today, the Internet, and search for the story of the Tuskegee Airmen, you would see the breadth of your influence in more than 7,000 pages of information that are on the World Wide Web. [Applause]

I think that is a tribute not only to your heroism, but to the impact you continue to have in shaping the attitudes of young people and creating an atmosphere that is favorable to progress and harmony among races. In today's military you are a force and a voice that commands attention and appreciation. And for that, we thank you. [Applause]

The Department of Defense—as many of you have heard this morning in briefings from my colleague and friend Bill Leftwich [Deputy Assistant Secretary of Defense for Equal Opportunity], and as others will talk about this afternoon—our department has a wide array of equal opportunity programs and policies today. It is a very dynamic area that involves many cross-cutting issues, and I am always appreciative to General Lyles, here as the Vice Chief of Staff of the Air Force in his previous job: a man who had held down in his previous assignment the most technically challenging job in America today, missile defense, with all of the skills in engineering, physics, [and] calculations. We'll always be grateful to General Lyles and the other Vice Chiefs for their leadership on their [Department of Defense] Equal Opportunity Council, a body that the Deputy Secretary of Defense chairs, [of which] Bill Leftwich is our executive secretary, and that has as its mission focusing to ensure that we follow your lead and keep those doors open, the doors of progress and opportunity.

But in these sessions, in these discussions, it is a very dynamic area that involves many cross-cutting issues. But the reason I wanted to come here today is really quite simple. I wanted you to hear directly a very important message about today's military. We have pride in today's military and we are proud of the strides that we have made, but we have not crossed the finish line. Indeed, in some ways our work is harder now because there are some who think that all of the issues have been resolved. You know and I know, that that is not true. The journey to opportunity has no finish line.

The Department of Defense has long been held up as a model for the rest of the nation on issues of race. In fact there has been more progress in the military than in the civilian world. Today's armed forces is the most integrated institution in America. More African Americans are in command, in leadership positions, than ever before—a fact that I think President Clinton and Secretary Cohen are particularly proud of. [Applause]

We have worked harder on this issue than any other institution, public or private. The practices and tones set at our bases and installations have had a strong, positive effect on the communities in which they are located. But that is only part of the story.

> *Today's armed forces is the most integrated institution in America.*

We can recruit young people from minority communities, but our job is not finished if those recruits move to less challenging fields because they lack skills and education when they come in the door.

Our job is not finished if we fail to recognize that each generation has its own unique problems and perceptions when it comes to race and ethnicity.

We can ensure our rules and regulations are clear and fair.

But our job is not finished if people believe that those rules and regulations are not being enforced fairly.

Our job is not finished if the rules and regulations work for those who are in uniform, but they do not reach people in our civilian workforce.

We can set strict policies against racism and discrimination.

But our job is not finished if there is a climate that discourages people from reporting harassment and abuses.

We can do everything possible to ensure that the promotion process is color blind.

But our job is not finished if men and women still lack mentors that can help them, guide them through those crucial hurdles at the O-4 and O-5 level, and at the mid-career and senior enlisted positions.

And our job is not finished if we are failing to present those with new tools and resources to those inside the military—ensuring that we reach out to them, rather than waiting for them to reach out to us.

Since your convention last year we completed two of the most comprehensive reports ever conducted on many of these issues: one on attitudes about race and ethnicity, another on promotions and advancement. We wanted to look beyond the numbers and find out about underlying causes and how these issues were perceived.

The positive news is that our men and women in uniform are doing better than the civilian society on issues of race. They are more likely to be friends with someone of a different race or ethnicity. They are more likely to socialize outside of work with someone of a different race or ethnicity. More than three-quarters have received some training on equal opportunity and discrimination issues in the last year. And despite a few isolated high-profile events in which the perpetrators have been pursued vigorously, hate groups and extremists barely register any presence in the military today. [Applause]

However, our work showed that there are still major differences in how issues of race and ethnic representation are experienced on a day to day basis. And minorities are much more likely than whites to see and appreciate that.

For example, minorities are still much more likely to have offensive encounters based on their race or their ethnic background. Minorities are still much more likely to be pessimistic about the future in race relations. Only 17 percent of whites believed that the armed forces have paid too little attention to issues of racism and ethnic discrimination. However, more than 60 percent of our minority members believed that too little attention had been paid.

We sometimes find that this is an uncomfortable topic to talk about. When General Lyles and Bill Leftwich and Ruby Demesme, [Assistant Secretary of the Air Force for Manpower, Reserve Affairs, Installations and the Environment] and I were assembled with the Vice Chiefs we found that the first issue was to not be uncomfortable talking about where we agreed, but also to be comfortable to talk about where we had different experiences. Because until we talk to each other, until we're ready to share those experiences, we can't begin to take the next steps toward that finish line that we're never going to reach. [Applause]

Another issue of particular relevance to this organization is the number of minorities in aviation. Always, every time I would see recently retired four-star General Lloyd "Fig" Newton, I'd like to tell him that when I would walk through the halls of the international airport in St. Louis there would be a picture of Charles Lindbergh and the *Spirit of St. Louis*, then there'd be a picture of Fig Newton, United States Air Force, Thunderbird pilot. If you ask Fig Newton who was the greatest fighter pilot he ever saw, without batting an eye he'd say, "You're looking at him." [Laughter and applause]

But you know, I also asked that question of Colonel McGee. [Laughter] He was talking about that P-51 going against the Messerschmitt and all of the maneuverability. I said, "Colonel McGee, who is the greatest fighter pilot you ever saw?" He said, "Well, you're sitting next to him." [Laughter and applause]

Our surveys have found that over a seven-year period from 1990 to 1997, there was an increase in the percentage of minorities moving into careers in aviation. But overall, the numbers need much improvement and we have much work to do there. America today needs all the pilots and aviators that it can find. There's a "help wanted" sign out there. So we've got to find everybody who has the tools and the skills and give them the training and the opportunity to sit there in the cockpit and take that F-16 or that F-22 or that Joint Strike Fighter to the top of the pyramid.

We're hopeful, and last year [Air Force] Secretary [F. Whitten] Peters addressed this issue. In fact our Air Force leadership is doing much by pushing to get more information into the hands of young

---

Fairness and opportunity for all cannot be afterthoughts of our military.

---

men and women who might not have considered the possibility of a career in aviation. In equal opportunity fairness, General Lyles would say there's opportunities in the Air Force space program as well, on the rocket side of the house as well as the fighter side of the house. There are cutting-edge jobs.

If you go to Patrick Air Force Base [at Cape Canaveral, Florida] and you meet the young majors and lieutenant colonels and colonels who are working on those Titans, and who are working on those Delta launch vehicles, and who are supporting NASA across the river at the Kennedy Space Center, you'll see that these are young folks of every race and ethnic group that are at the leading edge of the pyramid both on the flight line and in the launch site.

It's not enough, though, just to open the door to the armed forces. We have to make sure that everyone's voice is heard, and we have to know that everyone knows that we are in this together. Fairness and opportunity for all cannot be afterthoughts of our military. They have to be preconditions—at every rank and at every grade. Until that happens, we need to keep pressing. [Applause]

But the most important question is: Where can we move ahead and how? If we had exhausted every possible avenue of progress we could simply wait and say, "Every year 200,000 new young people come into the military—some of the here at San Antonio, at Lackland Air Force Base—they come into the military, and we can let time take care of the rest." That sounds easy enough. But the one thing we know about discrimination and racism is that it is never easy. It is never easy to talk about. It is never easy to confront. It is never easy to end. And it is always changing. The problems of today are in so many ways as difficult and complex as those of the past. So we cannot just wait on time. We have to use time.

That came to mind just a few weeks ago as I was thinking about these remarks and doing some reading. I was reading of World War II and all of the bravery of "the greatest generation" and the role that Judge William Hastie played. He was the Dean of the Howard University School of Law, the alma mater of, I think, General Lyles. He was an advisor appointed in 1940 to then-Secretary of War Henry Stimson. Later, in 1943, he resigned because he felt that on principle he had to resign over the treatment of the "Lonely Eagles" [the Tuskegee Airmen].

Surely he must have been filled with pride a few months later when he read that *New York Times* story of January 4, 1943. Judge Hastie was very critical of the military, but it's important to recall that he never gave up on it. He never stopped working for change. He continued to serve as a voice of conscience for the military and for the nation, pushing for change and condemning complacency but also praising those that had the courage to step forward.

As all of you know, five years later President Truman signed the order to begin a true integration of our armed forces. In 1948, President Truman personally thanked Judge Hastie for his role in speaking out for change, and speaking up for others who supported the change. In his plain, Midwestern way, Truman told Hastie, "I haven't seen you for several months now, but I know where you have been and what you were doing." Then President Truman said, "I just want to say thank you."

Ladies and gentlemen, you, the Tuskegee Airmen, have certainly upheld that great tradition of speaking up and speaking out in so many ways inside the service and inside America. You have served as warriors in the sky, as members of the greatest generation who faced in the very early years of your youth the rendezvous with destiny that changed the world. A grateful nation will always be in your debt. I thank you for that service. Thank you very much. [Applause]

II. Raising the Next Generation

Boys Are Born, Men Are Developed[1]

Be Great Enough So Others Trail You

James W. Compton

President and CEO, Chicago Urban League; native of Aurora, IL; graduate of Morehouse College; Merrill Scholarship to study French literature at the University of Grenoble in Grenoble, France; honorary Doctor of Humane Letters, Columbia College Chicago; serves on boards of Ariel Mutual Funds, Commonwealth Edison Company, and Field Museum of National History; affiliated with African-American Family Commission, Asian American Institute, and National Council of Negro Women; received the Living Legend Award from the African-American Youth Development Institute, the Thomas and Eleanor Wright Award from the Chicago Commission on Human Relations, and the Fred Luster Sr. Image Award by the Luster Products Black Heritage Foundation.

Editors' introduction: President James W. Compton gave this keynote address to 200 mentors, students, and parents active in the Carter Temple Mentoring Program in Chicago. President Compton insisted that children must be taught "the difference between needs and wants . . . between price and value." "Above all else," he counseled, "young African-Americans" should "be proud of who you are." The speech was "received quite well" and "prompted many questions."

James W. Compton's speech: Good morning, Mr. Glenn and all of the men and future men gathered here. I am honored to have been invited to talk to you today. While I know that you probably didn't invite any of the mainstream media to witness this event. They should be here. They should know that these types of programs exist in our communities.

Perhaps it would give them a different type of perspective, a better perspective, when they report on all of the things that are happening in African-American neighborhoods.

Somehow they often seem to miss the good and positive things. We need and deserve, not only a better balance in terms of what kinds of stories are done on our communities, but also more objectivity in the stories that are done.

---

1. Delivered in Chicago, Illinois, on March 20, 1999, in the morning. Reprinted with permission of James W. Compton.

One thing that concerns me is that there are not enough of these kinds of mentoring programs to fill the need. I see too many of our children out in the street at all hours seemingly without direction, and usually without any type of adult supervision. That is one of the best ways to get into trouble, and of course, they often do. And that's what we end up seeing on the 10 o'clock news.

I am pleased to see that many of the young men present are of elementary school age. At the Chicago Urban League we believe that intervention is most effective when the person is younger. If you wait too long, high school age and beyond, it is often too late to positively impact that young person.

As elders, we must come to grips with the fact that we face stiff competition in trying to gain the attention of our young men. There's television, radio, friends. . . and, in due time their heads will eventually be turned by the fair sex.

Back in 1950, long before any of you future men were born, the University of Michigan did a survey to determine what most influenced the actions and attitudes of young people. Not surprisingly, for those times, the results were: Home, School, Church, Peers and TV.

About 40 years later, in 1992 to be exact, a community-based organization did a similar poll of today's youth. Those findings, again not surprising given the times we live in, were: Peers, Rap, TV, Home, School and Church.

If we are to believe the results of this survey, home, school and church have less influence on today's youth than their peers, rap music and television.

There are several problems with this picture. First, if you are making important decisions about your life based on information from your best friend or someone from your peer group, you are seeking information from someone who may have less information and be less knowledgeable then you are.

I'm not an anthropologist, sociologist, or historian but I do know that traditionally knowledge and culture in most societies tend to be passed from the top down, that is, from the eldest to the youngest. The reason is obvious because it is the elders in our communities who have weathered all of the hard knocks of everyday life, and survived to talk about it and become role models. It is the elders who can help the young people avoid all of the many mistakes they made while growing up. And believe me, we have made many mistakes.

In the African-American community I am concerned because in many instances the young people seem to be in charge, not the elders. In many of our communities the elders actually live in fear of young people, particularly young black men. Go into many of our schools on the south and west sides and you'll find that the teachers and administrators are often afraid of the young people they are supposed to be teaching and developing into adulthood.

If we do not change this situation of young people running things, of culture being passed from the bottom up, instead of from the top down, I'm afraid that we just will not make it as a people as we take on the challenges of the year 2000 and beyond.

Second, while rap music is being acknowledged by many experts as a legitimate art form, it's just like any other kind of music. Some of it is good. Some of it is bad. Unfortunately the rap music that glamorizes the gangster life style and belittles women is among the most popular type of rap, and tends to give this whole category of music a bad name, particularly among people over 40 like many of the men in this room.

In the African-American community I am concerned because in many instances the young people seem to be in charge, not the elders.

While we are justifiably concerned about the possible negative impact on our African-American youth; I was surprised to learn that white suburban teenagers are actually the leading purchasers of gangster rap in this country.

The third problem with the results of this latest poll, is the fact that we have placed television in a position, so that instead of serving as a valuable source of information and entertainment, it often controls us. And African-Americans on average are the heaviest viewers of television on a daily basis.

Television, and particularly cable, can be a dangerous influence in your life if you allow it to control you instead of the other way around. I know some people who believe everything that they see on television. I'll ask how do you know that what you're saying is true? They respond, I saw it on television! No thought. No analysis. Just, I saw it on television.

And, of course, television is notorious for either the lack of African-American images, or the distortion of African-American images. There's nothing wrong with laughing, but do we really need so many black-oriented comedies? Is life in the African-American community really all that funny, given all of the serious challenges that we face on a daily basis?

Another problem that I have with television is that it historically has featured one-way communication. We sit there on a daily basis just soaking up information, and sometimes misinformation. I say historically, because with the new technology television is becoming more interactive with the viewer. This could be good for us. It could be bad for us if we don't control what has now become an even more powerful medium.

Television also poses a problem, particularly for those of us who are parents, because much of what young people think they want they first see on television. This can and has caused tension in many households because often parents feel that they have an obligation to their children to buy them material things that they see advertised on television.

Finally, the last thing I will say about the negative impact of television in our lives, is the fact that it forces our children to grow up too fast. By the time our children are teenagers they often have witnessed hundreds of murders and other violent acts, as well as every type of sexual activity imaginable.

> *The truth is that it doesn't matter how old you are if you have not learned some of the basics of what it takes to be a man.*

I think this phenomenon has something to do with the problems between generations in this society. By the time today's youngster is ready to graduate from high school they have had the same kind of visual experiences that previous generations didn't experience until they were much older.

The elders in the African-American community must do a better job of teaching our children the difference between needs and wants. You may want something that you see advertised on television; but as your parent it is my duty to advise you whether you need it or not.

Likewise, we must begin to teach our children the relationship between price and value. As a merchant in this free market society I can put any price on an item. Since I want to make as much money as possible, I will try to get you to buy the merchandise at the highest price possible. But what you pay for any given item does not necessarily have to do with its value.

I think that if we as elders pay more attention to some of these basic principles, we can do a better job of managing our financial resources and spend less money on things that we don't really need, and invest more in building up our families and communities.

All of what I have said so far leads me into my theme today that says simply: "Boys are born and men are developed." Somehow many of us in the African-American community have bought into the notion that becoming a man has something to do with how old you are.

The truth is that it doesn't matter how old you are if you have not learned some of the basics of what it takes to be a man. It's not automatic. There is a necessary and continuous period of development, nurturing and mentoring. Too often our children are just left to raise themselves, and never learn how to assume the awesome responsibility that goes with being a real man in this society.

Being a man means that you learn to accept responsibility for your actions. It means being able to say "I'm sorry" when you are wrong. It's learning how to reach down and help someone else make a way. It's understanding that you can gain more in this life by being cooperative rather than competitive.

It's being respectful to the women in your life. It's being willing to clean up and build up your community. It means contributing to your household, rather than always taking. It's understanding that being respectful and courteous are examples of strength, not weakness. It's understanding that it takes courage to feel so strongly about something that you cry. That's simply giving into the spirit that's inside all of us.

It's understanding that our community has raised up some sorry 40-year-old boys, as well as some magnificent 15-year-old men. Which will you be?

The 40-year-old boy is your neighbor who lives in the corner of his mother's basement and just can't seem to hold a job. Or if he holds one, it's not for very long. He's always borrowing money. He always seems to be cursing somebody out, usually a woman, and seems always involved in some kind of physical violence.

He lives from one day to the next and seems to always be blaming someone else for his problems. Everyone but himself. He went into a real deep depression when he realized a few years ago that as a single, able-bodied man, he would no longer be receiving welfare checks. In fact, one day he became so upset he dressed up and almost went out looking for a job.

The 15-year-old man, also your neighbor, is an overachiever. He's on the honor roll, while also holding down a responsible job. He's a volunteer tutor in his community. He knows who the gangbangers are, but he's smart enough to go his own way and make his own decisions.

He's often from a single female head-of-household family, and he has several brothers and sisters. You almost never see him just hanging out. He always seems to have purpose, and direction. He carries himself in a certain way that says, "I'm going to make my way in this world. And if you follow me you can make your way too."

He's a leader, not a follower. He's wise for his years, but not too wise to ignore good advice about his future. He realizes that there is honor in all types of work. He is a man of his word, and he always pays his own way, and sometimes your way, if you happen to be a little short that day.

He is a man of responsibility.

Future men, it's rough out here. Just when you think you've got things under control, something else happens. You have to learn to accept adversity as just another part of this puzzle called life. Everytime you're knocked down, you need to be thinking of how you're going to get up, even before you hit the ground. And then get up and move on.

Don't dwell on the bad times, because there are always more out there waiting for you.

Also, don't dwell too long on the good times, because there are always more challenges to meet.

No matter how smart or talented you are, remember there's always someone out there smarter and more talented. Take what gifts you have and improve on them. We all are gifted at something. Use your talents to help someone else, and you too will prosper.

And above all else, be proud of who you are. As young African-Americans you are unique. Look at how others imitate you. And because of all of the sacrifices of your elders there is nothing in this world that you cannot do.

Never fear to fail. And as a famous song once said, "Never walk in someone else's shadow." I'm saying, be great enough that others will want to trail you and walk in your shadow. You can be just that great.

Thank you for your kind attention. God bless and good luck to each of you.

Teaching Individual Self-restraint[2]

Taking Responsibility for Your Children's Actions

J. C. Watts Jr.

*Representative (R) to the U. S. House of Representatives from Okla-
homa, 1995– ; born Eufaula, OK, November 18, 1957; graduated
Eufaula High School, 1976; B.A. in journalism, University of Oklahoma, 1981; professional football player, Canadian Football League,
1981–86; member Oklahoma Corporation Commission, 1990–95, and
commissioner, 1993–95; received the Junior Chamber of Commerce's
Ten Outstanding Young Americans Award, the Jefferson Award for
promoting economic prosperity and free enterprise, the Christian Coalition's Friend of the Family Award, and the YMCA's Strong Kids,
Strong Families, Strong Communities plaque.*

Editors' introduction: Congressman Julius Caesar Watts, Jr., gave
this keynote address to members attending the National Rifle Association annual convention. Concerned about a "bizarre mentality" in the
United States that he believes "breeds anger . . . despair, and sometimes murder," Representative Watts urged delegates to "reach . . .
out to the many lonely and directionless kids in our communities."

J.C. Watts' speech: Thank you very much. It's very good to be
back with my friends from the NRA. I'm sure there are a few Second Amendment Sisters here as well. Good work, ladies.

I've said it publicly many times, and will say it once again: I am
the NRA. I am proud of the principles you are fighting for.

As is true of each of you, I make it a habit of citizenship to honor
the entire Bill of Rights, not just the Amendments that happen to
suit me. And let me restate once again that I stand completely and
forever opposed to allowing the criminal element to destroy our liberties.

These liberties, ensured by our Bill Of Rights, were properly recognized by our Founders as divine in origin, transcendent in
nature, and beyond the political manipulations of beings even so
powerful as talk show hostesses.

---

2. Delivered in Charlotte, North Carolina, on May 20, 2000.

My hope tonight is to talk about what I believe lies at the heart of our national violence problem, especially among our young people, and I also want to say a few words about the political debate raging over the issue of gun control. A debate that too often gets mired in superficial, simplistic arguments.

But first, I want to address the cultural issues. In a word, I believe our problem stems from a bizarre mentality that breeds anger, hopelessness, despair, and sometimes murder.

It is a bizarre mentality, but it is not an alien one. Quite the contrary. It is omnipresent and has, for many young people, replaced the mentality on which this nation was founded—a mentality that honored transcendent truth, personal responsibility, and duty to others.

American democracy was created for self-governing individuals— people who did the right thing whether or not anyone else was watching. It was created for people who honored the golden rule not because it was a rule, but because they understood that it truly was golden.

> *If we lose our ability to teach our children individual self-restraint, public order can only be maintained by outside forces.*

That mentality is under attack, and let me state my belief very plainly: If we lose our ability to teach our children individual self-restraint, public order can only be maintained by outside forces. In Washington last Sunday, we saw scores of thousands of Americans cry out for more laws. What they were really asking is for the government to protect us from ourselves.

That mass demonstration held a very clear warning. There are many, many Americans who are eager to exchange their constitutional liberties for additional security. And that, my friends, represents a crisis in confidence in the American experiment.

I now want to talk about what I believe are the most important Contributors to the bizarre mentality that affects so many of our children, a mentality that is robbing them of the ability to develop into self-governing individuals.

Let me be blunt. The first step we can take toward restoring our nation is for each of us to recognize that we, as individual citizens, have all too often drifted with the cultural tide that has brought us to this unhappy place.

We have not, for example, reached out to the many lonely and directionless kids in our communities, or even to our own kids.

We have left the television on in order to entertain and babysit our children.

We have succumbed to the easy role of trumpeting our beliefs at the expense of listening to others.

We have fallen for the sound bite mentality, which is a poor substitute for personal reflection and responsible action.

And as a nation, we have refused to accept the fact that we are now reaping what almost every one of us has sown.

Make no mistake.

We should not be surprised that some of our children are killing each other in our schools and on our streets.

We should not be shocked that many of our children have no sense of purpose, and feel hopeless and empty even in this era of unprecedented plenty.

We should not be surprised that, in the absence of the faith of our fathers, our children have adopted bizarre creeds, beliefs, and practices.

We truly are reaping what we have sown. And it is a very bitter harvest. We have all played a role in getting us here, and we all have a role to play in taking us home.

Let's look a bit more closely at how, we as a society, have created this bizarre mentality that affects so many of our children.

First of all, we have cut children free from parental authority. When I was growing up, when a parent said they were going to cut a switch, you suddenly knew the meaning of the expression "hell to pay." Nowadays, a kid responds by threatening to dial 911. Parental rights have been seriously eroded in many other areas, including how their children are schooled.

Parental authority has also been undermined by easy divorce and by public policies that have made fathers as rare as Steinway grand pianos in many inner city homes. As David Kopel pointed out in a recent essay, the biggest indicator of violence among young people is fatherlessness—no male influence.

Yet, interestingly enough, those gun-control marchers did not spend much time talking about those missing fathers. I don't want to rain on that parade, but it is surely ironic that those well-intentioned people came to Washington to pass laws that criminals will not honor—and were led by members of an entertainment industry that not only glorifies violence but which has promoted the sexual license and glorification of bizarre behavior which produces so many of our young violent criminals.

There is a frightful number of children growing up with very little parental discipline and guidance, which is crucial for helping them develop self-control and for feeling that they are loved and cared for.

No wonder so many look for love in all the wrong places. Those are often the only places left.

Our children have also been forced to live in a relentlessly secular culture. They have been robbed of much of their religious heritage by the complete banning of religion from public life, especially in our schools.

Don't think for a second that our kids haven't gotten the message. They can discuss almost anything in school except "Thou shalt not kill" and "do unto others as you would have them do unto you." Discussing the abiding truths of our Judeo/Christian faith makes the adults very, very testy—sometimes to the point of legal action. And that sends a very clear message to kids: Religion is either somehow bad or, at the very best, irrelevant to their lives.

Of course, I have something of a personal passion about this subject. As most of you know, I am an ordained minister. I believe that when these transcendent truths are driven from the scene, negative results will soon follow. I believe our contemporary history very much supports my assumption.

In fact, I feel very confident in saying that it is no coincidence that a society which undermines parental authority, which marginalizes religion, and which steeps its children in a violent and sexually obsessed popular culture produces children who are unruly, undisciplined, nihilistic, and in some cases infatuated with murder and quite prepared to act on these infatuations.

I am not saying that all our kids are bad. Far from it. For every bad kid who gets his picture on the cover of a national magazine, there are millions more trying to make their way in this world in a decent and positive way. They are working in school, and they are getting up in the morning wondering what they can do to make mom and dad proud of them.

But it only takes a relative few to cause an immense amount of damage.

It is also very clear kids aren't the only ones affected and infected by this bizarre mentality.

If any of you watched the gun-control march on television—I'm figuring not many of you were there in person—you might have seen a sign which said this: "Please protect us from guns." This sign told me that this protester has so misread the problem that she blames inanimate objects for crimes that originate in the human heart.

My view is vastly different, and was stated very well in a recent essay in *National Review* magazine. The writer of that essay made the point this way: Blaming guns for horrors such as Columbine is no different than blaming the chains for slavery. The problem isn't the guns. The problem is what is in the hearts and minds of the very small minority that decides to kill.

America has always been awash in guns. Why are more people, and especially young people, using them? I have mentioned weakened parental authority, easy divorce, and well-intentioned but harmful public welfare policies.

I am also fully convinced that our extremely liberal abortion laws have undermined the traditional bedrock view that innocent life is sacred.

Those of us born before *Roe v Wade* forget that every child born since 1973 knows that he or she could have been exterminated in his mother's womb with society's blessing. In other words, every American child knows that society considered him or her completely expendable. Anyone who believes that this does not cast life in a different light is, in my opinion, denying reality.

> *The problem isn't the guns. The problem is what is in the hearts and minds of the very small minority that decides to kill.*

In fact, if there is one cause that brings more celebrities to the Mall than gun control, it is abortion.

Which finally brings me to our entertainment industry. Let me be very clear. Our entertainment industry creates many wonderful works. Some are nothing short of astounding. My kids and I watch *Beauty and the Beast* over and over.

But this industry also bombards our children with epics of blood, sex, and nihilism. Some are overt, such as Oliver Stone's *Natural Born Killers*. Others are much more subtle.

And there is no doubt in my mind that children are getting the message.

I don't know how many of you have looked at the police report on the Columbine massacre, but it points out that the killers, Eric Harris and Dylan Klebold, were very deeply affected by the movie *Natural Born Killers*. Klebold, for example, wrote an entry in Harris's yearbook that said, "the holy April morning of NBK." NBK of course stands for "Natural Born Killers." Harris wrote something very similar in Klebold's yearbook. Again, I quote: "God I can't wait till they die. I can taste the blood now—NBK"

Let me give you two more quotes. One is from a school notebook, and is thought to have been written a day before the attack. Here's what it said: "About 26.5 hours from now the judgment will begin. Difficult but not impossible, necessary, nerve-wracking and fun. What fun is life without a little death? It's interesting, when I'm in my human form, knowing I'm going to die. Everything has a touch of triviality to it."

Here is the other: "My wrath for January's incident will be god-like."

Let me make a couple of points. You will note, for one thing, that the killers had filled their spiritual vacuum by making a religion out of violence. Their high priest seems to have been Oliver Stone.

I am not guessing here. We have the killers' word for it.

Yet the entertainment industry will not accept any degree of responsibility.

Now folks, this is an astounding position. What Hollywood is telling us is that children are not affected by what they read, see, and hear. This is obviously wrong and any parent who has to buy Pokemon cards, Beanie babies, Nike shoes or Cookie Crisps knows better.

Can we link the Columbine slaughter to the entertainment industry? Clearly, we can. If a person is caught painting swastikas on a synagogue, and then a subsequent search of his room discovers Nazi literature, don't we assume a link? Of course we do.

Similarly, if a person attacks a citizen of a different race, and a subsequent search of his home finds racist literature, don't we assume there is a link? We would be incredibly foolish not to.

Now, let's look more closely at Columbine.

According to the police report, Klebold and Harris hoped to kill hundreds of classmates by detonating bombs in the school cafeteria. Those bombs were in fact planted, but they did not go off, and I'm thankful to the good Lord for that, because the police report says 480 students could have been killed if the bombs did detonate.

We can only imagine the horror. As Timothy McVeigh showed us, bombs can do a great deal more damage that guns in a much shorter time.

Interestingly enough, I don't recall hearing anyone blame the Ryder truck, the fertilizer and ammonia that McVeigh used to build his bomb for that horrific crime. Quite the contrary. The president blamed anti-government rhetoric and talk radio. Not many people, at least on the gun-control side, disagreed. They were admitting that people can be inspired to violence by their cultural experiences.

After the Columbine killings, police searched the killers' homes. What did they find?

They discovered hate literature, violent video games, and writings by the killers showing a deep affection for the work of Oliver Stone.

But who has gotten the lion's share of blame for this horror?

The man most to blame, we have been instructed, is Charlton Heston.

Of course, the entertainment industry knows that people are affected by what they read, see, and hear. Hollywood makes a great deal of money by merely placing certain products within camera range, knowing that some viewers will be influenced by this most passive sort of advertising.

More to our point, producers and actors are quick to take credit for sensitizing audiences to the causes dear to their hearts, many of which are quite noble. I truly believe, for example, that the entertainment industry played a positive role in improving race relations in our country.

And the time has come for some in Hollywood to admit that while it can inspire people to do good, it can also inspire people to do evil. And if it continues to create these films, it should pay a price.

Am I suggesting censorship?

Not at all! Those of us gathered here tonight understand that our freedoms are indivisible. Some folks believe they can whittle away Amendment 2 without threatening Amendment 1, but they are wrong. If Hollywood's First Amendment rights can be taken away, so can your Second Amendment rights.

What we can do, however, is expose and denounce those who pump rot into our society. We just call them what they are. They are cultural polluters. They are playing a central role in the corrosion of our children's character, and they should no longer get a free ride.

And excuse me for a few moments while I put on my Republican hat and say a few words about the political debate going on today.

It's an election year and the rhetoric is getting pretty hot. The Vice President and many of his Democrat colleagues on Capitol Hill are weighing in. But, in the whirlwind of their overblown rhetoric and partisan politics, they are no where close to the root causes of these problems we are confronted with.

In fact, gun control consistently finishes at or near the bottom of the list of solutions to youth violence. Eighty-four percent of those polled believe that greater involvement by parents in the lives of their children would have the greatest impact on reducing gun violence in our schools.

Over the last thirty years, we have slowly become a culture that says the only thing right is to get by, the only thing wrong is to get caught; if it feels good, do it; if you don't want to do it, don't; if you don't like it anymore, divorce it; if it's inconvenient, abort it; and, if you can't handle it, drink it or drug it.

And yet, it is this same culture where our children spend more time watching television and playing video games before they are 8 years old than they will spend with their parents their entire lifetime.

Just like you, I believe in sensible gun safety laws, but not in an attempt to impose morality from without as a substitute for parental instruction, which instills morality from within.

I wish I could believe that proposing more gun control measure would or could do more to protect our children. But, time and time again, even newly proposed gun legislation would not have kept these acts of violence from happening.

Numerous current gun laws were broken at Columbine and many other well-known shootings. Yet, we ask ourselves: would another gun law truly have made a difference?

Washington, D.C. has some of the most restrictive gun laws in America, but none of them were able to keep a recent shooting from occurring among local teens at the National Zoo. Yet, Vice President

---

I believe in sensible gun safety laws, but not in an attempt to impose morality from without as a substitute for parental instruction, which instills morality from within.

Al Gore took the opportunity to call, once again, for handgun safety trigger locks.

Many were quick to point out the obvious, that a disturbed kid breaking the law would NOT have had a safety lock in the first place.

It's gotten to where anytime the Vice President is informed of a shooting, he calls for child-safety trigger locks, even if children were not involved in the shooting.

His motives are to instill fear in Americans as he talks about "illegal guns flooded our communities" and yet wants to require licenses for all law-abiding gun owners. Yet, just ten years ago, A1 Gore was voting against these types of gun control.

Vice President A1 Gore is the type of politician where nothing is sacred, that will say and do anything to Preserve their own political future, even if that means using fear and deceptive means.

His party used to say, "there's nothing to fear but fear itself." Now the Vice President has nothing to offer but fear itself.

Friends, it is up to us to put America back on the right track of preserving the Constitution and away from the cultural decay we are currently in.

First, we must work toward stronger enforcement of our current gun laws. Our current Administration has a dismal record of gun enforcement and has shown little in way of making it a priority.

Under the Gun-Free School Zones Act, for example, the 6,000 students caught at school with a weapon in the past two years could have all been prosecuted. How many did the administration actually prosecute? Just 13.

There are some ideas that we must pursue legislatively if we are to reverse the direction toward cultural renewal. We must work to return control of our schools to parents and communities, helping parents make the right decisions about what's best for their children's education, and provide for the inclusion of faith-based schools.

Secondly, we must provide for real pro-family tax relief and letting families keep more of their own money. It is wrong for both parents to have to work, spending less time with their children, purely to pay the family's tax bill.

Also, I believe we must do more to help parents and educators find the help for those kids who exhibit the early warning signs of violence and self-destruction.

This current cultural decay has taken decades to form and changes today may not be realized for years to come. But we must for the sake of our children and for our children's children, move our culture closer to one that prizes strong families, promotes positive cultural influences on our children, and reaffirms the inclusion of faith-based organizations.

And lastly, we must send a clear message to Al Gore and all politicians that they do not hold all of the answers to solving all of the problems within our society. We must tell them to stop looking for the "quick fix," and pointing their finger at the easy target.

We must reject "made-for-television" legislation sold to us by politicians, promising to keep these tragedies from happening again, but are only truly concerned about furthering their own political future.

And we should call on the entertainment industry, many of whom protest guns by day and promote gun violence by night, to take more responsibility to promote gun safety instead of the bizarre, warped, and ultimately irresponsible gun use they promote in TV, video games and movies.

In these final few moments let me return to my earlier theme. Yes, it is necessary to identify the contributing factors to the bizarre mentality that has hurt our children. But the first step on the long journey toward restoration must take place in our own hearts and homes.

Nobody should expect Washington, or Hollywood, to say No More until they say No More in their own homes.

Let me ask a personal question. How many of you fear future Columbines? You don't have to raise your hands, but I think it's safe to say we all fear the possibility. Now, let me ask another question: Why do you fear that such a horror may be repeated?

I believe that all Americans, if they are honest with themselves, do not fear future Columbines because there are too many guns in America—or, for that matter, because there are too many propane tanks from backyard barbecues, which is what Klebold and Harris used to make their bombs.

I think the reason this fear nags at us as a nation is because we know our own children and our neighbor's children have been raised in the same culture that produced these two young men.

We may even wonder if our own children are capable of perpetuating such horror.

And while the focus is rightly placed on children, we must never forget that we, as adults, have created the world our children are being raised in.

It is not our children who make the movies, video games, and television shows.

It is not our children who have driven God from the schools.

And our children are not responsible for the moral free-fall in our public and political institutions. We are. You think our kids aren't getting the message?

I have said before: I am a man of faith, and a man of hope. I believe we know the way back. And I am convinced that our journey begins in our own hearts and homes.

But I am convinced that if we do not take those steps, and the others that naturally follow, then the people who are all willing to exchange their liberty for security will win the day. And to be quite frank, they will deserve to. We must run with perseverance the race that is set before us.

And so, my friends, we find ourselves together with a long, hard journey ahead. There is nothing less at stake than the American experiment in ordered liberty, and the lives of our children.

But I am convinced that we can prevail. If we do our best, our best will suffice. The strength of America is not our guns or Hollywood or government—the strength of America is our people—you, me, us, other Americans, our hopes, dreams ambitions, our ideas and most important our goodness.

Thank you, and God bless each of you.

Saying Yes to the Children[3]

The Faces of the Future

Leo J. O'Donovan, S.J.

President, Georgetown University, 1989– ; born New York City, April 24, 1934; summa cum laude, Georgetown College, 1956; advanced degrees in theology and philosophy from Fordham University, 1961, and Woodstock College, 1966; ordained to priesthood in the Society of Jesus, 1966; doctoral degree in theology, University of Munster, Germany, 1971; taught theology at Loyola College, Maryland, 1961–63, Woodstock College, 1971–74, Weston Jesuit School of Theology, Cambridge, MA, 1974–81, and Georgetown, 1981–89; past president, Catholic Theological Society of America; former associate editor of Journal of the American Academy of Religion, *1985–89; contributed to* Ex corde Ecclesiae, *Pope John Paul II's Apostolic Constitution on the nature and role of the Catholic university, and* Evangelium Vitae, *the Pope's encyclical on moral issues of life and death; has received numerous awards and honorary degrees from organizations in the U.S. and around the world.*

Editors' introduction: Reverend Leo J. O'Donovan gave this Closing Keynote Address at a luncheon that concluded the Child Welfare League of America's National Conference on Children 2000: Face of the Future. He praised the delegates present, claiming, "In each face of suffering," they "help inspire or create a face of love, a face that is the future." "We must stand together," President O'Donovan maintained, "and demand that this country provide more support for parents and communities so that we can raise happy and productive children." Mark Rowland, a social worker mentioned in Fr. O'Donovan's speech, was honored posthumously at the conference.

Leo J. O'Donovan's speech: Thank you. It is a great pleasure to join you today and a special honor to have been invited to participate in the Child Welfare League of America's annual conference, "Children 2000: Faces of the Future." I am particularly grateful to be here with the League's new director, Shay Bilchik; Deputy Director Shirley Marcus Allen; members of the CWLA Board, today's honorees, and all of you who so proudly celebrate the commitment that brings us together—our commitment to supporting our children's bright and productive future.

---

3. Delivered in Washington, D.C., on March 3, 2000. Reprinted with permission of Fr. Leo J. O'Donovan.

Caring for the future has always been at the heart of activities of the Child Welfare League, the nation's oldest and largest association of agencies devoted to improving life for children and families. And it is at the heart of Georgetown University, America's oldest Catholic university. While I am not an expert in child welfare, I share with each of you a sacred vocation—a special calling to serve others. Today I want to speak about why that calling is so important and particularly why what you do is critical to the well-being of communities across, this country.

In your efforts to provide loving homes for abused and neglected children, decent housing and food for families in need, a second chance for troubled teens, each of you is dedicated to building stron-

---

Ours is an age-old challenge to find new ways of saying yes to our children—to affirm their great capacity to grow and to be.

---

ger futures for children and their families. And each of you knows that caring for the future means caring for "the faces of the future." People—not statistics, not facts, not professional goals or organizational challenges—people are the center of what you do and why you have come here. You understand that in every person you care for—the wailing infant, the homeless child, the pregnant teen—you care for all humanity. In each face of suffering, you help inspire or create a face of love, a face that is the future.

In caring for children, you are part of a strong tradition that reaches back more than one hundred years in this country. In fact, a little more than a century ago, America's earliest child welfare advocates gathered in this city amid one of the worst blizzards ever to attend another annual conference dedicated to ushering in "the century of the child." Conferees were made of sturdy stuff indeed, and the conference's host, the National Congress of Mothers, reported proudly that "not a single speaker failed to appear," and that the pews of the First Baptist Church at 16th and O Streets were filled to capacity.

What spurred these people to risk life and limb in a snowstorm that would make present-day Washingtonians quake? They wished to exchange ideas about the best ways to foster the growth of children, to prepare them for complex responsibilities in a changing world, and to discuss how to implement a new "child-centered" conception of family life and apply the medical advances of a new field called pediatrics. Most of all, they were drawn by the conviction that what they did mattered tremendously to the well-being of the communities in which they lived, and further that independent, educated, and healthy children were the foundation of a stronger nation for the next century. The women and men who attended this conference were in many ways our ancestors in child advocacy, and their can-do spirit and fierce determination is alive in this room.

Today we face many of the same challenges of those caring adults of 1899, especially the challenge to understand and better provide for children; to seek new ways to reinforce children's diverse interests and aspirations; and to affirm the special capacity of children to learn widely, feel deeply, and imagine expansively. Ours is an age-old challenge to find new ways of saying yes to our children—to affirm their great capacity to grow and to be.

And that challenge is ever-daunting. You know better than I the problems facing individuals and institutions dedicated to caring for children. Every day in America:

Nearly 2,200 babies are born into poverty;
More than 1,300 are born without health insurance;
Nearly 13 children die from gunfire;
More than 2,700 students drop out of high school; and
More than 1,300 teens get pregnant.

You know the facts. But focusing on the dire import of these statistics can sometimes lead us to view children as a collection of problems, not as people who possess great potential and are assets to our communities.

I want to tell you a story about a man named Anthony Motley and the importance of saying yes to children. As a high school sophomore, he was involved in an inter-racial fight with other students at school, and subsequently was called to the principal's office. The principal explained that for his behavior Anthony would be expelled from school. That's, right: Anthony made a mistake and tried to resolve a conflict with a fist fight, and the punishment for his mistake was removal from a place of learning. This did not happen in Illinois in 1999, but here in the District of Columbia in 1965 . . . and that's not the end of the story. The principal also stated that he would see that Anthony was not only expelled from his high school, but from every high school in the city.

Anthony's father along with the family's pastor interceded and convinced school authorities to give him another chance, not to give up on him. As a result, Anthony was able to enroll in and graduate from another local high school. He went on to be the first in his family to earn a college degree, a B.A. from the University of Detroit. He has served in our nation's armed forces, and he earned a Master's of Divinity from Howard University, proudly becoming the Reverend Anthony Motley. In 1987, President Reagan appointed him as special assistant to the federal government's non-profit domestic volunteer agency.

Reverend Motley is also an active child advocate working with youth in his community through an organization called Inner Thoughts that he co-founded in 1991 with his wife. In collaboration with Catholic Charities, Inner Thoughts supports youth in South East Washington, D.C., by providing summer camp opportunities, after-school programs, and clothing for their everyday and business needs. It is a wonderful organization, touching the lives of more than 125 young people in the community each week and more than 1000 each year.

Reverend Motley's story is a story of triumph. But at each step, it could have gone another way if he had not had people in his life who were willing to say yes to his development: The father and mother who said, "yes, you deserve an education . . . ." The army sergeant who said, "yes, you should further your interest in community outreach and pursue an advanced degree . . . ." The elderly woman whom he met while volunteering at a rally against economic injustice, who said to him, "yes, young man, you are special . . . you can reach people." Each step of the way, Reverend Motley had someone who made a difference, who supported him and believed in him, who saw him as a person of possibility, not a problem. He had, as well, God's protection and is indeed in his own way another incarnation of God's yes to us, as the Bible puts it.

Each of you here—child advocates, grassroots organizers, foster parents, kinship caregivers, policy makers—each of you makes a difference in the lives of the children you work with and for. You work each day to say "yes" to children's health and safety, "yes" to a loving home life, "yes" to their education, and "yes" to their bright future. By saying yes, you not only foster children's futures, you help create that future.

But it's certainly not easy. As we know from the courageous examples of those honored today, especially Mark Rowland and his wife Lynette, saying yes to children can mean taking great risks—even the risk of your life. The situations you face are often not clear-cut, not black and white. You are frequently called upon to make tough and complex decisions, to reach past even the best training in your field to find solutions. On any given Monday, in your role as child advocate you may be called upon to help:

The 18 year-old who needs to adapt to the new and daunting responsibilities of a completely independent adult life on his own after foster care support ends; or the mother who has lost her home and needs to find a new one before she is charged with neglect and loses her much-loved children; or the child in foster care who is about to return to her original family.

Armed with research, experience, faith, and good judgement, you seek the best solutions. And you know that each situation demands special understanding and special consideration of who, not what, is at the heart of the issue—a child. You know every case demands someone who can say yes to a child's future:

Yes, we can find you and your family a safe place you can call home;

Yes, we can help you get medical treatment for depression;

Yes, we can help you understand your mistakes and learn from them;

Yes, we can work to eradicate violence in your life;

Yes, we can help you find rewarding part-time work;

Yes, we can help you pursue the best education and opportunities for self-improvement;

Yes, we believe in you;

Yes, we will hold your hand and pray with you.

Each of you in the diverse organizations that make up the Child Welfare League of America is saying yes in many ways and saving children's lives every day, but as you know there is much more still to do. Engaged as we are in the passionate struggle to save a single abused child, a single teen mother, a single runaway young person, we must also find collective strength in our work.

We must stand together and demand that this country provide more support for parents and communities so that we can raise happy and productive children.

We must demand that the entertainment industry offers and promotes programming that lifts the souls of the young—programming that doesn't mesmerize them with visions of violence, but affirms their aspirations.

We must demand that the tobacco lobby stop marketing cigarettes to children and stop putting health beneath the bottom line.

We must demand that our government say no to guns, no to the violence that has resulted in the U.S. leading industrialized nations in the number of youth homicides.

We must demand that federal and state governments mend the holes torn in the safety net in 1996 after passage of the Effects of Personal Responsibility and Work Opportunity Reconciliation Act and the holes torn in the fabric of community as office seekers have played politics with people's lives.

We must demand access to excellent classes, after-school activities, part-time jobs, sports teams, internships—not just things to do, but opportunities which allow our young people, the future of our country, to imagine a future for themselves.

Speaking up, saying yes—it sounds simple. But as you know it demands a great deal from each of us. It demands courage and fortitude and imagination. It demands faith . . . .

And it's exhausting. To say yes, as one French playwright reminds us, you have to work hard and "sweat and roll up your sleeves and plunge both hands into life up to the elbows."

As you leave here today to dive once again into the varied, complex, and high-stress work of caring for children and families, let me offer some brief words of advice. More than a century ago educators spoke of the 3 R's needed to build a child's education. Today I would like to offer you the 6 R's to guide you in your work in advocacy: rely, reach out, reflect, respect, receive, and remember.

RELY on others. Don't try to do everything by yourself. Take the time to renew the friendships you have formed here this week, to reconnect with those in your family and in your hometown.

REACH OUT to others in your community. Caring for children is a common cord shared by those in many occupations—in teaching, parenting, preaching—so do not hesitate to forge new relationships, to reach out to the school or church or even a single family across town or next door to invite collaboration or to share ideas. The most common excuse for community inaction is "No one ever asked me to help."

REFLECT. Take time for personal reflection—time to renew the commitment you made when you entered your profession and dedicated yourself to the service of children and families.

RESPECT the power of your own influence. Through your work, you are models for children and as models you have great and enduring influence. Adults, indeed, will see the world differently because of you. But children will have a world because of you.

RECEIVE from those you seek to help. Albert Schweitzer once noted that "giving is the only valuable process." He advised us wisely to impart as much as we can of our spiritual being to those who are on the road with us. But he also advised that we receive as precious the many gifts that come back to us—the gift of a child's smile of self-confidence, the girl of a warm handshake of gratitude, the gift of inspiration that comes with another newfound beginnings.

And, finally, REMEMBER that your work is the Lord's work. You are living a message of love for one's neighbor, the most vulnerable among us—a message and a vocation, which lies at the heart of every great religious tradition and is the heart of our shared future together. In saying yes to children, you make a promise as powerful as any marriage vow, a promise borne of hope, fulfilled in hope. And in saying yes to children, you say yes to their creator.

Thank you.

III. Domestic Politics

U.S. Trade Policy and the Trading System[1]

Charlene Barshefsky

U.S. Trade Representative, 1997– ; specialist in international trade law; B.A., University of Wisconsin, 1972; Doctor of Law, Columbus School of Law at the Catholic University in Washington, D.C., 1975; partner in Washington, D.C., law firm of Steptoe & Johnson, 1975–93; Deputy U.S. Trade Representative, 1993–96; acting U.S. Trade Representative, 1996–97; led the negotiation for Information Technology Agreement, Agreement on Basic Telecommunications, Financial Services Agreement, and commitment from all World Trade Organization members to the principle of "duty-free cyberspace"; achieved a historic bilateral market access agreement with China on the terms for that country's accession to the WTO, 1999.

Editors' introduction: Ambassador Charlene Barshefsky addressed 100 graduate students, faculty, administrators, and guests in the Silver Auditorium at the Graduate School of International Economics and Finance at Brandeis University. The speech was part of the CEO Forum Speakers Series sponsored by the Sy Stewart Distinguished Lecture Fund. In the speech Ambassador Barshefsky assesses the United States's "commitment to open markets, freer trade, and the rule of law in world commerce." The U.S. "trading system," she maintained, must not only serve our own interests but those of the "world's poorer countries." After the speech, Ambassador Barshefsky took questions for about 30 minutes on the role of trade in the U.S. economy, U.S. Trade relations with Africa and China, and other topics.

Charlene Barshefsky's speech: Thank you very much. Let me begin by recognizing Peter Petrie, a distinguished trade scholar, and also Mickey Schulhof. I am very pleased to be here with Ira Shapiro, who throughout the past decade has been both a shaper of American trade policy and a close friend—and who I want to have introduce me at every speech from here out. And equally, I am very happy to meet and exchange ideas with so many of the young men and women who will guide New England and our country as businesspeople, activists, analysts and policymakers in this new century.

---

1. Delivered in Waltham, Massachusetts, on April 13, 2000, at 11:00 a.m. Reprinted with permission of Ambassador Charlene Barshefsky.

We have a full trade agenda: China's membership in the World Trade Organization and permanent NTR; regional initiatives in Europe, Africa, Asia, the Western Hemisphere and the Middle East; legislation to strengthen trade ties with Africa and the Caribbean; a newly begun negotiations at the WTO on agriculture and services. But rather than focus on any one of these issues, or give you a laundry list of agreements and export statistics, let me today put our agenda in its context: our role in developing the trading system now embodied by the WTO; the values and aspirations we bring to this work; and the tasks we face in this new century.

AMERICAN TRADE PHILOSOPHY

Our work at the WTO, to begin with, rests upon a foundation of American commitment to open markets, freer trade, and the rule of law in world commerce.

Americans have taken this position for over a half century. In one sense, this is a matter of economic logic. Open markets abroad enable us to export, and exports are essential to a strong domestic economy. Almost 80% of world economic consumption, and 96% of the world's population, is outside the U.S.; foreign tariffs and other trade barriers

Imports help American workers specialize in the most technologically sophisticated and financially rewarding fields.

are substantially higher than ours. As markets open more fully to Americans, farmers face less risk of gluts that drive down prices, workers see opportunities for higher-wage employment, and firms gain economies of scale that help them invest in plants, jobs, and research.

Open markets here at home are equally important. Imports create the choice, price and competition that raise family living standards—for all families, but most especially the poor—and help to dampen inflation. Accompanied by commitment to education and job training, imports help American workers specialize in the most technologically sophisticated and financially rewarding fields. And they give businesses access to inputs—raw materials, parts, business equipment—that reduce costs and thus improve efficiency and competitiveness.

But our work has rested on more than economic logic: for over half a century, it has had a base both in practical experience with the alternative; and in our broader values and aspirations. And to understand why, we can trace our trade policies back to the beginning.

HOOVER AND ROOSEVELT

Our modern trade policy begins, essentially, with the debate between Herbert Hoover and Franklin Roosevelt in the Presidential campaign of 1932.

President Hoover's trade policy had rested on the belief that America, with its high standard of living, could not compete effectively with poorer countries. As Hoover put it, in a message to Congress in 1929 calling for passage of the infamous Smoot–Hawley Act, we "cannot successfully compete against foreign producers because of lower foreign wages and a lower cost of production." He persuaded Congress that he was correct and the result remains well-known today: a cycle of tariff hikes and retaliation which cut trade by 70% between 1930 and 1933, deepened the Depression, and intensified the political tensions of the era.

Roosevelt proposed the alternative, which we have followed ever since in principle and put broadly into practice after the Second World War. As he put it in 1944:

> A basic essential to peace, permanent peace, is a decent standard of living for all individual men and women and children in all nations. Freedom from fear is eternally linked with freedom from want. [And] it has been shown time and time again that if the standard of living in any country goes up, so does its purchasing power—and that such a rise encourages a better standard of living in neighboring countries with whom it trades.

In 1948, when President Truman and 22 of his colleagues joined to form the WTO's predecessor (the General Agreement on Trade and Tariffs, or GATT), they were attempting to transform this insight into a lasting set of policies and agreements. This was one in a series of policies and institutions that have served us ever since:

- Collective security, reflected by the United Nations, NATO, the Rio Treaty and our alliances with the Pacific democracies.

- Commitment to human rights, embodied by the Universal Declaration on Human Rights and a series of more recent Conventions.

- Open markets and economic stability, with the creation of the IMF and World Bank on the one hand, and the foundation of our modern trade policies in the General Agreement

Truman and his colleagues believed that by reopening world markets they could rebuild a shattered world economy; restore economic health and raise living standards; and that over the long term, together with a strong and confident security policy, as open markets gave nations greater stakes in stability and prosperity beyond their borders, a fragile postwar peace would strengthen.

This is in fact what has happened. Through eight Rounds of negotiations, and as 112 new members joined the 23 GATT founders, we abandoned the closed markets of the Depression; and the results are clear. Those countries which participated most fully in the work—first in Western Europe, then Southeast Asia, Latin America and Central Europe—have seen living standards rise and political tensions diminish. Those which have done less—the Middle East, South Asia, Africa—have seen poverty persist and political instabilities at times intensify; but today these regions too are moving toward policies that stress integration and shared benefit.

In broader terms, the opening of world markets has helped foster a fifty-year economic boom. Since the foundation of the GATT, and our building upon it through the creation of the WTO in 1995, trade has expanded fifteen-fold; the world economy grown six-fold; and per capita income nearly tripled. As a result, hundreds of millions of families escaped from poverty, and this is clear in statistics of social progress: since the 1950s, world life expectancy has grown by twenty years; infant mortality dropped by two-thirds; famine receded from all but the most remote or misgoverned corners of the world; and the openness of our own economy has helped to power America's economic success in this decade.

THE WORLD TRADE ORGANIZATION

Where do we go from here? In thinking about trade policy and globalization today, let me suggest four points we should consider important:

First, we need to pursue a course that ensures the strength of our own economy. There is nothing wrong in this: in fact it is central to your own future.

Second, it is not enough that the trading system works for us. It is a moral imperative that it also advance the integration and development of the world's poorer countries.

Third, we need to ensure that our other important values are maintained—trade is not everything, and economic growth by itself is not enough.

Fourth, trade policy—especially in the aftermath of the Cold War—is a central means of building the international relationships that cement peace.

The WTO can and should be one instrument in responding to each of these important considerations. And let me take each in turn, briefly.

I. STRENGTHENING THE AMERICAN ECONOMY

First of all, the WTO is an institution which promotes the open, confident policies initiated by Roosevelt, and thus, helps us to strengthen our own economy and improve life in the United States. And it does this in several ways.

1. Opening World Markets

To begin with, it has helped us to continue opening markets and creating opportunity worldwide.

In creating the WTO, we eliminated quotas and industrial tariffs by a third; broadened coverage to areas the GATT covered only partially or not at all, notably agriculture, services and intellectual property rights. And we are now going on to the negotiating agenda of the next decade. Its core elements are before us, in the agreement last February to open global talks on agriculture and services. In these sectors markets remain most distorted and closed, and thus the opening of trade means perhaps most to future prospects for rising living standards, technological progress, and sustainable development. And in each we have ambitious goals.

We are now also examining market access concerns in industrial products, electronic commerce, trade facilitation, and other topics as well. One especially important, and universally recognized, need is for the WTO's wealthier and more advanced members to open their markets more fully to the products of the poorest and least developed nations. And the WTO is exploring ways to take the next steps in such areas as investment and antitrust policy, which are connected to trade but are not yet subject to their own multilateral regimes. Thus, while there are a number of different options for proceeding with trade liberalization beyond the agricultural and services sectors, we are continuing our work to build consensus for a new, more broadly based Round.

2. Strengthening the Rule of Law

At the same time, and apart from the negotiating agenda, our economic strength depends on the rule of law. And the WTO has strengthened the rule of law.

The GATT system had a limited set of essentially unenforceable rules that applied differently to different members. With the WTO, we have a more comprehensive set of rules that are enforceable and apply to every single member, with transitions. Together with this are an array of oversight bodies to monitor the commitments our trading partners have made; and a strong dispute settlement mechanism which we have used in 49 cases to preserve and enforce our rights.

This is of fundamental importance. The cases in which we have been involved, of course, help us to protect American rights and give individual Americans fair treatment when it has been denied. Through the dispute settlement process we have, for example, proved our contention that Canada was unfairly subsidizing exports of dairy products, hurting the livelihoods of dairy farmers in Vermont; and we protected American musicians against copyright piracy in Japan. And as they secure these concrete and specific interests, they help us confirm more basic principles: WTO members must keep their commitments; trade policies must be nondiscriminatory; we and other trading nations have a fundamental right to set the highest standards of environmental protection and consumer safety—an absolute right confirmed in a number of dispute settlement decisions.

3. Building The 21st-century Economy

In the WTO we also created a permanent forum in which governments find new areas of shared interest and benefit, which we used in the past five years to reach four agreements of central importance to the 21st-century economy:

- The Information Technology Agreement, eliminating tariffs on $600 billion worth of trade in high-tech manufactured goods such as computers, semiconductors, computer equipment, integrated circuits and telecom equipment, and so forth, on which we are now building toward an ITA II with still broader product coverage;

- The Agreement on Basic Telecommunications, opening world markets in a sector dominated for 60 years by monopolies and promoting pro-competitive regulatory principles. In just two years, it has eroded the ability of dominant carriers in foreign countries to keep rates artificially high and depress demand for telecommunications services and electronic commerce, helping to bring down rates to levels as low as 10 to 20 cents per minute, for calls between the U.S. and countries such as Japan and Mexico;

- The Financial Services Agreement, covering nearly $60 trillion in financial transactions—a figure half again as great as total world GDP—per year. It has already helped U.S. services suppliers expand commercial operations and find new market opportunities both through ownership of or investment in foreign banking institutions, brokerage and insurance sectors, and through cross-border trade.

- And the WTO's commitment in 1998 to "duty-free cyberspace," helping to make sure electronic commerce develops freely as a means to promote trade, strengthen the power of consumers, and help the most impoverished regions take advantage of world markets.

4. Prosperity and Economic Security

Altogether, this makes the WTO an institution of great practical economic benefit.

We see this in our own economy, as the opening of world markets has helped spark a 55% expansion of American goods and services exports since 1992, to a record total of $958.5 billion last year. Together with—and inseparable from—domestic policies including fiscal discipline and investment in education and job training, the opening of world markets has contributed to a remarkable record. If you will pardon a few statistics: we have seen $2.1 trillion in economic growth, during the longest economic expansion in American history; the creation of nearly 21 million new jobs; a $400 billion expansion in our manufacturing industry; wages for non-supervisory up; poverty rates at the lowest levels since 1979; and unemployment touching 4% in January, with record lows for women, African-Americans and Hispanics.

And just as important as these positive figures is what Arthur Conan Doyle in one of his Sherlock Holmes stories called "the dog that didn't bark." That is, in the Asian financial crisis of 1997–99, with 40% of the world in recession and five major Asian economies contracting by 5% or more, the world faced a crisis unlike any since that which sparked the great Depression in the 1930s. But in this crisis, WTO members generally remained true to their commitments; affected nations had the access to markets necessary for a speedy recovery; and the political strife that can erupt in economic crisis never emerged.

This is a remarkable tribute to the work of the past seven years, and the foundation of the past fifty: the world in the 1990s passed a test it failed sixty years earlier. And if the GATT founders were here to see the results of their work, they could be forgiven for taking considerable pride in it.

II. PROMOTING DEVELOPMENT

Second, the WTO is an opportunity to spark development and integration for the world's poorest countries.

This is not, of course, a task that trade policy can do alone. It must of course be matched by appropriate domestic policies in the least developed countries. And on the international scene, in many least developed countries, the financial burden posed by debt has made growth very difficult; and President Clinton has thus challenged our Congress and the world to forgive 100% of this debt when relief will help finance basic human needs. But these nations also need access to markets, especially in areas of comparative advantage, and at times technical assistance to implement the market access commitments through which they attract investment and gain exposure to modern technologies. And we have developed a response.

We are enhancing our market access programs, beginning with expansion of the duty-free GSP program, and going on to more ambitious legislative proposals like the African Growth and Opportunity Act and expansion of the Caribbean Basin Initiative. The WTO is central to our efforts to win approval for similar and broader commitments worldwide, joining other industrial nations and the more advanced developing countries.

Equally crucial, we are helping these countries participate more fully in the system. Many of them come to the table with less experience in trade policy and at times fewer resources to devote to it; they thus often feel they have difficulty in asserting their rights and interests in the WTO. A proposal we introduced last year, together with Bangladesh, Lesotho, Nigeria, Senegal and Zambia, to improve the technical assistance and capacity-building programs available from the WTO and other international institutions, can serve as a starting point.

III. PROTECTING OUR VALUES

Third, the WTO has an important part to play as we think about the questions of the quality of life—sustainable development and environmental protection; equity for working people; transparent and accessible institutions. These are as central as the unfinished work of opening markets and advancing the rule of law. And as we approach the task, we can draw important lessons from our experience at home.

Since the last time our unemployment rate touched 4%, in January of 1970, our economy has grown from $3.7 to $9.2 trillion, manufacturing output nearly tripled, and 50 million men and women joined the work-force. This is nowhere more evident than in Boston, with the high-tech economy it has built in these years. At the same time, the percentage of our rivers and streams fit for fishing and swimming doubled, as one can see with a walk down the Charles River; many endangered or threatened species are recovering, as we can see with the return of the Atlantic salmon and the bald eagle to New England; we created modern consumer safety laws and key regulatory policies; and the number of workplace deaths fell 60%.

More recently, as our economy opened further with the trade agreements of the 1990s, we also wrote a stronger Safe Drinking Water Act, strengthened clean air standards and protection of wild lands; passed the Family and Medical Leave Act; and raised the

---

There is absolutely no reason the world economy of the next decades cannot see the same combination of growth, better environmental protection, safer factories, stronger labor protection, and job creation.

---

minimum wage. And despite fears that a more open world would reward countries with lower wages or weaker labor and environmental standards, America's share of world foreign direct investment rose sharply, with foreign countries investing well over $500 billion in America between 1994 and 1998.

Clearly, those who fear a "race to the bottom" can take reassurance in these facts. As our economy opened and grew in the past decade, our domestic labor and environmental standards have improved. But we also believe that there is absolutely no reason the world economy of the next decades cannot see the same combination of growth, better environmental protection, safer factories, stronger labor protection, and job creation. And while the principal driving forces for these changes are, of course, domestic policies, the trading system also has a role to play.

1. Environmental Protection

It can do more to help us protect the environment.

Here the work has begun reasonably well. The WTO already cites sustainable development as a fundamental goal, and its agreements explicitly recognize the fundamental right of all its members to set any level of environmental protection, conservation and consumer safety desired, including at higher levels than international norms.

Looking ahead, we have a series of proposals for trade liberalization with direct environmental benefits: elimination of barriers to trade in environmental goods and services; as well as fishery subsidies which contribute to the world overcapacity that has endangered the Grand Banks among other historic fishing grounds; and agricultural export subsidies that increase pressure on land and water. And last fall we established a broad framework for systematically integrating environmental concerns into our trade negotiations, through the President's Executive Order on the Environmental Review of Trade Agreements, and the White House Policy Declaration on Environment and Trade.

2. Trade and Labor

It is also true that the WTO can address more effectively the concerns of many workers.

Today, in a formal sense, the WTO does not recognize that links between trade and labor exist. This is not a position which can endure: it is intellectually indefensible, and it will over time weaken public support for the trading system. Our task, therefore, is to ensure that the WTO formally recognizes the relationship between trade and labor policy and acts upon it.

This is not by any means easy: many developing countries—democracies such as Brazil, South Africa—raise genuinely felt concerns that such a discussion would lead to discrimination against the poor. Our work must recognize and allay these concerns if we are to make progress. But while there are no easy answers, all of us will ultimately benefit from such a discussion.

3. Transparency and Institutional Reform

Finally, the WTO must fully reflect the basic principles of openness and transparency which are essential to the success of any institution.

As trade grows and the impacts of globalization intensify; as trade becomes more important to all nations; and as improving education and modern telecommunications open all institutions to ever greater scrutiny and debate—the need for openness, accountability and public access is greater every year.

The WTO does not yet fully meet this test, and that is, ultimately, a challenge to its future. Thus we are working for greater transparency throughout the system, through the progressive attainment of some practical goals: ensuring rapid release of documents, enhancing the input of citizens and citizen groups; providing the opportunity to file amicus briefs in dispute settlement proceedings, and opening those proceedings to public observers. These are essential to public support for the institutions of government at home; and the same is true for the institutions of the trading system.

IV. END OF THE COLD WAR

Fourth and finally, the WTO is of cardinal importance in our response to one of the great political challenges of the present: the end of the Cold War, with the opportunities it creates to support reform in the countries from Central Europe to Southeast Asia breaking with strict communist planning systems; and thus to strengthen peace.

This is a task for our time with consequences as great as those of the GATT's reintegration of Japan and Germany in the 1950s. It is highly complex: in technical trade policy terms, the transition economies have features unlike most of those we have encountered in the past; and it is still more complex because in political terms they have chosen different paths, some emphasizing political change and others delaying or hoping to avoid it.

Thus it proceeds slowly and with occasional setbacks. But it is also achievable and well underway. Since 1995, the WTO has admitted six transition economies: Slovenia, Bulgaria, Mongolia, the Kyrgyz Republic, Latvia, and Estonia. Georgia will enter soon; and the accessions of Albania and Croatia are almost complete. We have made significant progress with Armenia, Lithuania and Moldova; and held fruitful discussions with Russia and Ukraine as well.

And in our bilateral agreement on WTO accession with China, together with permanent Normal Trade Relations, we have an opportunity of vast consequence. This is a comprehensive, one-way agreement covering agriculture, services, industrial goods, unfair trade and investment practices and other rules, with specific, enforceable commitments in each area. Together with extension of permanent Normal Trade Relations, it will open China's markets in a way unprecedented since the 1940s, creating new opportunities for American farmers and businesses as it strengthens our guarantees of fair trade.

As with the foundation of the GATT, its potential beyond trade may be still more important as a spur to broader economic and social reform in China, and as a means to deepen and strengthen a process that has helped China become a more responsible member of the Pacific community. That is leading advocates of democracy and human rights in Hong Kong and China—Bao Tong, jailed for seven years after Tiananmen Square; Ren Wanding, a founder of

China's modern human rights movement; Martin Lee, the leader of Hong Kong's Democratic Party—see this agreement as China's most important step toward reform in twenty years.

CONCLUSION: THE WORK AHEAD

That is our record in fifty years of leadership in the trading system: one of helping to create opportunities and raise the living standards of Americans; of spurring development and growth worldwide; of advancing American values; and of building a stronger peace.

But it is also true to say that the trading system can be improved—the WTO is a product of human effort, compromise and negotiation; and everything human is flawed by definition. All of us, and young people in particular, should always look at the policies and institutions of the present and ask how we can do better. The WTO and its members must be open to new ideas and listen to its critics; only through openness will it retain the broad support of the public and its member governments over time.

But as we take up the challenge of reform, we must also remain true to the values and aspirations that animated Roosevelt and Truman at the foundation of the trading system. The generous and far-sighted project they began has helped to spark an era of growth and rising aspirations unmatched in human history; has played its part in stabilizing peace; and can do still more in the years to come. The task will be by no means easy; but as we think about the work ahead we should be optimists, remembering always that others before us have shouldered equally difficult tasks and always brought them home to success.

Thank you very much.

Latino Voters[2]

The New Political Landscape

Arturo Vargas

Executive Director, National Association of Latino Elected and Appointed Officials (NALEO) Educational Fund, 1994– ; born El Paso, TX, 1962; graduate of Stanford University and Stanford University Graduate School of Education; Vice President for Community Education and Public Policy, Mexican American Legal Defense and Educational Fund, 1993-94; 1991 Redistricting Coordinator, MALDEF, 1990–93; 1990 Census National Program Director, MALDEF, 1988–90; Senior Education Policy Analyst, National Council of La Raza (NCLR), 1985–88; member of Boards of Directors of Independent Sector, National Immigration Forum, Edward W. Hazen Foundation, Hispanics in Philanthropy, National Civic League, Multicultural Collaborative, and National Hispanic Leadership Agenda, authored reports and articles on education and Latino political development.

Editors' introduction: Executive Director Arturo Vargas spoke to the Center for the New West's Annual Western Political Outlook Forum, "Hot Spots, Wedge Issues and Front Runners: New West Presidential Politics," at the Boardmoor Hotel. In this two-day seminar, 120 political scientists and journalists focused on the 2000 presidential elections. In his speech, after reviewing the scope, nature, and impact of Latino votes in the United States, Mr. Vargas concludes that "the candidate who can best convey a message to Latinos on the most important issues that they care about will have the advantage." The speech was very well received.

Arturo Vargas' speech: Thank you for inviting me to be with you here this evening, and to speak about a topic that I think is very timely: the role of Latinos in American politics. And I have to tell you, it is somewhat frightening to see two white, middle aged men speaking better Spanish than your own niece and nephews. [LAUGHTER]

Yet I believe it says a great deal about what is happening today with respect to Latinos and American politics. There are (and I do this for the benefit of my friends in the media) five main points I want to make with respect to this topic.

---

2. Delivered in Colorado Springs, Colorado, on September 29, 1999, 7:00 p.m. Reprinted with permission of Arturo Vargas.

First, the impact of Latinos in the electorate is largely based upon the increase of Latinos in the general population.

Second, there has been a steady and consistent increase in Latino participation in voting since 1992, and much of this has been a result of a significant contribution of new citizens, newly naturalized citizens, who have had a demonstrable impact on the Latino electorate and their behavior.

Third, the political hostility toward immigrants and Latinos contributed to the increase of legal permanent residents applying for U.S. citizenship and participating in voting, which set the stage for an overwhelming support for Democrats from Latinos from 1994 through 1998.

Fourth, the concentration of Latinos in strategic states make their role in the Presidential election very important.

And, lastly, the next election will be a true test of whether this trend of increased Latino voter participation, holds, and also will be a major opportunity for the Republican Party to make up some lost ground with Latinos.

In 1990, the Census Bureau counted 22.1 million Hispanics in the continental United States. When we (NALEO) count the number of Latinos in elected office, we include only the 50 states. We do not include elected officials in Puerto Rico. The 1990 census represented a 50% increase over 1980. Half of this increase was due to immigration. Half of that increase was due to natural factors, the difference of births or deaths.

Two weeks ago, the U.S. Census Bureau released population growth estimates from 1990 through 1998, and reported a 36% increase in the Latino population during this period. About 7.9 million Latinos were added to the U.S. population. Latinos now account for about 11% of the U.S. population, and in about five years, Latinos are expected to surpass African-Americans and become the second largest population group in the United States.

Latinos are a large and growing population as well as incredibly diverse: 63% of U.S. Latinos are of Mexican origin, about 14% of Puerto Rican origin, 6% are of Cuban origin, and about 12% are of Central and South American origin.

In the West, the Latino population is overwhelmingly of Mexican origin with a strong and growing Central American population, particularly in California. In fact, Los Angeles has the largest concentration of Salvadoreños of anywhere outside of El Salvador. Second only to Washington, D.C., and followed by Houston. The Latino population's diversity also is geographic. Latinos live in each of the 50 states, yet we are concentrated in a handful of states. Latinos also are incredibly diverse politically, which I will discuss shortly. Latinos are also a youthful population, which has a fundamental impact on Latino voting strength. Nationally, Latinos have a median age of about 26 years, compared to a median age of 36 years for the Anglo population in the United States. Thus, of every 100 Latinos, 40 of them are unable to vote because they are under 18. Of the remaining 60, about 40% of them, can not vote because they are not U.S. citizens. And when issues such as low levels of educational attainment, low levels of income, and low home ownership rates, are factored in, it is not hard to understand why 5% of the U.S. electorate is made up of Latinos while the U.S. population is 11%. Thus, when people claim, "Well, Latinos don't vote," this represents, I think, a lack of understanding about the nature of the Latino population. Often, Latinos do not vote because they can not vote. Many are too young and many others are not citizens. Now, the age factor will adjust over time. The citizenship factor has been changing, and I will talk about that in a few seconds as well. Yet despite these factors that inhibit voting, there nevertheless has been a steady and consistent increase in Latino voting strength.

In 1992 about 4.2 million Latinos voted, accounting for about 3.7% of all voters. In 1994, 3.5 million Latinos voted, less than in 1992, but such a decrease is typical of an off-year election when there was no Presidential race.

This decrease is expected among all population groups, yet the percentage of the electorate that was Latino went up, 4.1% of all voters. The 1996 election represented an historic rate of Latino voter participation. That year, there were 6.6 million Latinos registered to vote and just under five million voted, representing 4.7% of the overall electorate. About 1.1 million of those voters were in California. Figures of 1998 are still based on estimates and exit polls and Census Bureau has not issued data yet, but the common wisdom is that 5% of the electorate in 1998 was Latino.

How did Latinos vote? Well, in 1992, 65% voted for Clinton, and 25% for Bush. 1994 was the year of the Republican landslide, . . . but it also was the year of Proposition 187 in California, which I believe really became the defining moment for Latino politics this decade.

The initial impact was that in California, Latinos matched their voting performance in 1994 as in 1992. In other words, as many Latinos voted in a non-Presidential election year in 1994 as voted in Presidential year in 1992. Every other population group experienced a decrease, as they do in every non-Presidential race. 1994 was the exception for Latinos.

While Latinos still voted less than what their eligibility rates would suggest, 1999 represented a new direction for Latino voting patterns. In addition to marking historic rates of voter participation, 1996 also was marked by new milestones and an infusion of new voters.

About 700,000 more Lations voted in 1996 than in 1992, while the number of non-Latinos voting declined in absolute numbers. Thus, a phenomenon which is occurring is that as more Latinos are voting, more non-Latinos are not voting, which increases the overall Latino percentage of the electorate and makes the impact of Latinos so much stronger at the voting polls. 1996 also was the election that saw the strongest Latino support for a Democrat candidate. Clinton received about 71% of the Latino vote, while Dole, received 21%, the lowest for a Republican candidate.

And there is a gender gap among Latinos, just as there is among non-Latinos. Eighty percent of Latinas voted for Clinton, and 60% of Latinos voted for Clinton. Fifty-three percent of the electorate in the Latino community is made up of women; the gender gap is even more pronounced among Latinos than among non-Latinos.

Of course, there were many milestones that occurred in 1996 that many of you already have heard about. The election in the 46th Congressional District in California was a major victory for Latinos, with Loretta Sanchez, who is now considered a hero in the Latino community defeating incumbent Robert Dornan by 984 votes. Here, David slew Goliath.

There was an overall increase in the number of Latinos serving in Congress which included the addition of Rep. Silvestre Reyes, the first Latino to represent the E1 Paso area of Texas in Congress. Even more significant was the Latino voting performance in a couple of key states. In Arizona, 80% of Latinos voted for Clinton, and Clinton carried that state. In Florida, 44% of Latinos voted for Clinton, and Clinton carried that state. In those two states, Latinos had a demonstrable impact; they made a difference for the Democratic candidate.

How Latinos voted in 1996, I believe, is related to who were the Latinos who voted. Shortly after the 1994 election, there was an unprecedented increase in the number of legal permanent residents applying for U.S. citizenship. In fact, in April of 1995, the Los Angeles Immigration and Naturalization Service (INS) District Office was receiving 2,400 naturalization applications a day. In 1995, just under half a million new citizens were sworn in. In 1996, just over one million new citizens were sworn in, 36% of them in California. One out of seven new citizens sworn in 1996 were in Los Angeles.

There can not be such a tremendous infusion of new citizens and new voters without having some kind of an impact. In 1996, 31% of all Latino voters in Southern California were first time voters, and of these, 72% were naturalized citizens.

Naturalized citizens are having a real impact on who Latino voters overall are. Many observers of Latino political behavior who have been following these trends in the Latino community believe that the increase in the interest in naturalization is a reaction, in fact, to Proposition 187 in California and to the welfare legislation passed by Congress in 1995 that denied benefits to legal, permanent residents. Not undocumented immigrants, but to legal, permanent residents.

Many of these citizens during this period of overt hostility toward immigrants, and Latinos specifically, sought out U.S. citizenship, I believe, as an act of self-defense, out of anger, out of fear, and out of a real desire to play a role in politics. And they have had an impact on the Latino vote overall. Eighty percent of the new voters voted for Clinton and only 5% of the new voters voted for Dole.

According to the Tomas Rivera Policy Institute, 75% of Latinos who voted that year in the L.A. area voted to support Democrats, but only 16% say they voted to punish Republicans. Yet 63% believe that Governor Wilson's proposals on illegal immigration reflected his racism toward Latinos. We at NALEO conducted a survey of over 1,000 Latinos who had applied for U.S. citizenship between 1992 and 1995. We asked them what were the most important reasons why they were applying to become a U.S. citizen.

Ninety-six percent of them said that the most important reason was to vote; 73% of them said to keep benefits. Interesting thing was that of those who applied in 1992, 72% said it was important to become a citizen to fight discrimination against Latinos, but in 1995, 87% of them said it was important to become a citizen to fight discrimination against Latinos. Thus we have seen a great infusion of new citizens who are voting, and they are voting with a mission. A new U.S. citizen is often more American, and more interested in participating in American politics, than native born citizens. In fact, they are outperforming native born Latinos, and in many areas they are outperforming native born non-Latinos in their rates of voter registration and their rates of voting.

I would like to share a personal story with you. My parents are from Chihuahua, Mexico, and I was born in El Paso. My parents moved to El Paso in 1952. My folks moved to L.A. in 1964, and in 1993 my mother decided to apply to become a naturalized U.S. citizen. At her swearing-in ceremony, there were about 6,000 other applicants crowded into the L.A. Convention Center. All of them were waving miniature American flags and, this is one of the things that I'll admit the INS does right; it makes it a special, emotional event.

Afterwards, I asked her, "Mom," and of course all of this is in Spanish. "Mom, why did you finally decide to become a U.S. citizen?" "Well," she said, "there were two reasons. One, because all the work that you've done," and I thought to myself, "Oh, finally, she gets it."

Then I asked her, "Well, what was the second reason?" It does not translate that well from Spanish to English, and she used more colorful language, but in essence she said, "Because I want to vote against (Governor) Pete Wilson."

This, I believe, was the motivation that drove those hundreds of thousands of Latinos who applied for U.S. citizenship fight after the November 1994 election.

A new generation has emerged, although not necessarily permanently, a generation of Latino voters who vote religiously and vote to support Democratic candidates. In the 1998 elections, Latino support helped in Congressional, state legislative and statewide races throughout the State of California and in the West. Again, the Tomas Rivera Policy Institute reported that Wilson's high negatives among Latinos really dragged down Republican candidates. In fact, in a 1997 special election for a state legislative race in a heavily Latino and heavily immigrant district where all the candidates were Latinos, the one who won in a landslide used the message that he was the best candidate to oppose Pete Wilson's policies.

Now, he was going to be one of 80 members of a legislature, but his campaign was, "I'm the best one to go up against Pete Wilson," and he won in a landslide in a Latino district.

Gubernatorial candidate Gray Davis also was a huge beneficiary of the Latino vote. Eighty-one percent of Latinos voted for Davis; 77% of Latinos voted for U.S. Senator Barbara Boxer. Cruz Bustamante, the first Latino to win a statewide race since 1871, was elected Lt. Governor.

GOP gubernatorial candidate Dan Lungten received 20% of the Latino vote, despite the fact that he did everything he could to distance himself from Pete Wilson and spent a great deal of money advertising in Spanish on television and radio, and mailing campaign literature in Latino communities. His outreach did not work because the memory of Pete Wilson was much, much too strong. This trend has continued in the increase of voters. At the same time, again, that we are seeing the overall voting rate of non-Latinos decreasing.

Three Latino candidates also beat Republican incumbents in the California state legislature. One in Orange County, one in the Bakersfield area, and one based in Pomona, in eastern Los Angeles County. We also saw the election of Latino mayors in the City of Salina, the City of San Jose, and Congresswoman Loretta Sanchez came back and, once again, beat Bob (Dornan). This time, though, by 56% to 39%.

The coattails of Latinos spread beyond California as well. We are here in a state (Colorado), one of only four states, that has elected a Latino to statewide office: Ken Salazar, the Attorney General of the State of Colorado, a Democrat.

New Mexico has a long history of electing statewide candidates. That state currently has six statewide Latino elected officials.

A critical element in producing Latino voters is organized labor. I encourage you to look at the role of labor unions in not just organizing Latinos to join labor unions, but organizing Latinos to turn out at the polls. Unions have had a demonstrable impact on California races and could be pivotal in the 2000 election.

Of course, there are notable exceptions to the Latino Democratic landslide, obviously George W. Bush in Texas is one of these exceptions. There are estimates that he received anywhere from 39% to 49% of the Latino vote in 1998. Some argue that Latino turnout in Texas was low to begin with, so it was only his hardcore supporters who turned out. So the percentage of Latino support that Bush received may not necessarily represent his strength throughout all the Latino community. Yet the bottom line is the Governor is popular among Latinos in Texas, and he had coattails as well. Tony Garza won statewide in the State of Texas as a Republican, and he now sits on the Texas Railroad Commission. California elected three Republican Latinos to the State Assembly, joining the one who was elected in 1996. There are now four Latinos in the Assembly who are Republican, and 13 who are Democrat. And there are two caucuses: the Latino Legislative Caucus that is Democrat, and a Hispanic Republican Caucus. Great diversity for the community that I think is very healthy.

When you step back one year, back to 1997, another Republican candidate who did very well among Latinos is Mayor Riordan of Los Angeles. He received a majority of Latino support and 48% of Latino voters were first time voters. Here was a situation where new voters who support Democratic candidates were supporting a Republican incumbent mayor in a local race.

There is another election going on right now, also in Southern California, to replace the late George Brown in Congress. In the primary, State Senator Joe Baca was the Democrat who came in first, and he could very likely become the 19th Latino in Congress today. So that is another development to keep an eye on. What is interesting about this race in San Bernardino County is that it is a fairly conservative blue collar district—in the Inland Empire that is far east of the City of Los Angeles. Joe Baca is a member of the NRA. He is a conservative Democrat. He probably will play very, very well in that district.

Of course, the focus of the Latino vote today is the potential impact on the elections of next year, and the concentration of Latinos in several strategic states make them an important calculus for whoever intends to win a majority of the Electoral College. Ten states with significant Latino voting populations have about 80% of the Electoral College votes needed to win the White House. These states include Massachusetts, Illinois, New Jersey, Florida, New York, Texas, and out here in the West, California, Arizona, New Mexico and Colorado. Latinos are about 12% of the voters in California, 11% in Arizona, 33% in New Mexico, and about 8% in Colorado.

California, of course, with 54 electoral votes is a vital state, which explains why both Al Gore and George W. Bush are spending an awful lot of time in California. Arizona Senator John McCain is also somebody who has been very, very popular among Latinos in the State of Arizona, and he is seeking out Latino venues. It is no surprise that these candidates are speaking Spanish and seeking to address Latino voters.

The Republican strategy is really to try to get at least 40% of the Hispanic vote. If Republicans get 40% of the vote, they believe they will have been successful. They claim that they are going to work hard for the Latino vote. They are going to put money into TV ads, something that we have not seen nationally since the 1998 race between George Bush and Michael Dukakis. Bush is attractive to the Latinos. He has a base in Texas, and his brother (Gov. Jeb Bush) is very popular among Latinos in Florida where he received 67% of the Latino vote. Bush is also consciously distancing himself in California from Pete Wilson. I have yet to see George W. Bush and Pete Wilson in the same room, and to me it is no surprise. George W. Bush opposes English Only. He supports vouchers, which in fact are popular among Latinos, and he has worked well with Hispanic leaders in Texas.

Many Latino elected officials in Texas who are Democrats are hard-pressed to really criticize George W. Bush as somebody who has not looked out for the interests of Latinos on some issues. So he is doing something fight in terms of reaching out to Latinos in the State of Texas. The big question is, will he play outside of Texas?

You may have heard about the controversy this summer where Bush was invited by three national organizations to address them at their annual meetings: the National Council of La Raza, LULAC, the League of United Latin American Citizens, and NALEO, the National Association of Latino Elected And Appointed Officials.

It really was puzzling to me why he decided to skip each of our three conferences. Each of us draw significant media attention. Each of us draw significant and different niches of the Latino community. Yet to each one of us he claimed to have scheduling conflicts.

I think, however, that he is being strategic in which Latino venues he seeks out. He was in California twice recently. Once to speak at the Latin Business Association conference, and then in San Diego to speak at the conference of the US Hispanic Chamber of Commerce. I think he is being very strategic in which Latino venues he selects, selecting those where he believes he will have a receptive audience. He also believes he can win California. Again, he, and Republican strategists believe that he needs 40% of the Latino vote to win the state, and I think he can actually do it.

Bush's biggest liability, though, I believe, is his Party's leadership in Congress. A recent poll by Univision, the Spanish language TV network, indicated that Latinos support Democrats in Congress 66% to 24%, and they disapprove of Republicans in Congress 50% to 39%. And Congress is doing things, as Congress can do, that are not to the benefit of Latinos, and frankly, I think that they could be a huge liability for Bush.

House Speaker Dennis Hastert, for example, has not made himself available to meet with the National Hispanic Leadership Agenda, an organization which I chair. It is a coalition of 32 national Latino organizations. We met at least twice with Speaker Newt Gingrich, and we agreed to disagree on some issues, and on some issues we found common ground. Yet, since he took office, Dennis Hastert has not been able to make time to meet with the CEOs of the 32 largest national Latino organizations, something that is baffling to me.

I think the debates over the Census and sampling were harmful to the Republican Party. The Census is an issue that is very keen in the Latino community. Latino organizations and Latino leaders made the census a priority in 1970, 1980 and 1990, and we will again in the year 2000.

Latino organizations and leaders are engaging in comprehensive outreach efforts to educate Latinos about the importance of being counted in the Census. Whenever anybody puts himself in the position of appearing not to advocate for a full Census count, it sends a strong message to Latinos that you are not on their side.

There are a couple of other issues before Congress this session that also could hurt the image of the Republican party among Latinos. The restructuring of the INS is being proposed in a way that my organization opposes—my board of directors, which is 20% Republican—opposes. Congress is proposing to cut funds for bilingual education, which has strong support among Latinos.

I think these actions in Congress are not helpful to Bush, and I believe Bush is doing all he can not to associate himself with members of his Party who are in the Congress, and in the Senate. The Senators have done a very poor job of confirming Latino judicial candidates, which is probably the most important issue we in the Latino community have before the U.S. Senate. Judge Richard Paez from California, who has been nominated to the Ninth Circuit, has been waiting for three years and 10 months to be brought forward to a floor vote. He has been reported out of committee, but he is being held up by a couple of Senators and not being brought to a vote. This is an issue that many of us in the Latino community are following very, very closely.

Nonetheless, I think the Republicans can make headway among Latinos, who do support some traditional Republican themes. The Univision polls show that Latinos strongly support school prayer, they support vouchers, but they also support Medicare, health care reform, education, education funding, and affirmative action, which I think gives Gore and the Democrats the opportunity to distinguish themselves from the Republicans.

Gore is very well known among the Latino community. He has had an infrastructure for the past six years to reach out to Latino leadership and Latino elected officials. He will need every one of them to inspire Latinos to go out and vote for him. The big question is the Bradley factor. Obviously the race between Bradley and Gore is tightening. Bradley is largely unknown to Latinos. I do not know a single Latino elected official who has endorsed Bradley.

I recently had a long conversation with an individual who works in the Bradley campaign who was lamenting the fact that there are no Latinos involved in the Bradley campaign infrastructure, and that Latinos are supporting his candidacy. His message to me was that Latinos had better get on the bandwagon, because Bradley is going to win and Latinos would be left out if Latinos are all with Gore.

Well, if Bradley intends to carry California, he needs to start reaching out to Latinos. The Bradley factor may be a very interesting wrinkle in the Democratic strategy to try to carry states like California and to carry the Latino vote. The most recent polls in California among Latinos still show an edge for Gore over Bush. Gore, 54%, Bush, 37%, and there are other polls that suggest Gore at 49%, Bush at 24%. But remember, success with Latinos for the Republican Party is getting 40% of the Latino vote.

The *L.A. Times* poll put Bush at 37% support among Latinos. It is within reach.

The big question is, will the trend of voter participation among Latinos continue in the year 2000? There are some indications that the factors contributing to low voter turnout overall, the good old American political apathy, may be catching up to Latinos and affecting them as well.

The sting of Proposition 187, welfare reform, Proposition 227 may be fading. And other than in Arizona, where there is another initiative to eliminate bilingual education, there do not seem to be emerging other wedge issues that may be galvanizing Latinos like they were in 1994, 1996 and 1998.

Ultimately, I believe, the candidate who can best convey a message to Latinos on the most important issues that they care about will have the advantage.

The most important issues for Latinos today are crime and drugs, education, and economic opportunity. Look for continued outreach to new voters. Look for the use of Spanish language media to reach these voters.

As the Presidential race unfolds, Latinos are settling into position where we have worked very, very hard to be. We want to be in a place where our vote is not taken for granted by Democrats or Republicans; where candidates consciously reach out to Latino voters and work hard to convince us that they offer the better alternative to advance our interests, and that political parties think twice about pursuing policies that will alienate Latinos.

This is essentially where we want to be. We are not there yet, but I think we are well on our way. Thank you.

Star Trek's Lessons for the Disability Community[3]

Adapting to Change, While Holding onto Values

Sue Suter

President of Suter and Company in Springfield, IL; former president of the World Institute on Disability and former director of the Illinois Department of Children and Family Services.

Editors' introduction: Ms. Sue Suter addressed delegates to the Annual Conference of the Association for the Severely Handicapped, including "people with disabilities and families and professionals and advocates." The conference was sponsored by the Illinois chapter of TASH, an international association of people with disabilities, members, other advocates, and professionals concerned with human dignity, civil rights, education, and independence for all individuals with disabilities. Believing that "the world needs to rediscover what's normal," Ms. Suter states that "people with disabilities are ordinary people." She ends with this challenge: "Will our action steps create the world we want?"

Sue Suter's speech: Thank you for this honor, and for making this day one of the highlights of my life.

In a new book called *Quotable Star Trek,* Jill Sherwin uses thousands of quotations to encourage people to think about their lives and the lessons they can learn from this popular series. Today, I want to share some of those lessons with you, as we open this conference on systems change.

The first lesson from *Star Trek* comes from one of television's first leading characters to be portrayed as having a disability—the blind chief engineer, Geordi Laforge.

In a scene where LaForge is confronted by a culture that euthanizes its members with disabilities, he answers:

Who gave them the right to decide whether or not I should be here? Whether or not I might have something to contribute?

---

3. Delivered in Springfield, Illinois, on September 12, 1999, Springfield, Illinois. Reprinted with permission of Sue Suter.

Who has the right to judge whether people with disabilities belong? People have been raising their hands for centuries. From Greek philosophers who endorsed the humane disposal of disabled infants over cliffs, to 1940s German purification policies, to declarations by today's elites.

One example can be found in a September 7th *Newsweek* column by George Will about Princeton's new professor of Bioethics. The teachers name is Peter Singer, and he noted for advocating a utilitarian approach to children with disabilities. This includes applying utilitarian calculations to determine whether a disabled child's life should be spared, based on the painful life they might face and costs to society for keeping them alive.

He also advocates letting parents consider the option of infanticide of a severely disabled newborn. This to relieve them of the burden of caring for a disabled child, and to allow them to replace the child with a normal baby that would certainly enjoy a happier life. Part of our battle is to fight the mentality that says the greatest goal is the perfection of the human race. And we see that message in the most common of places. Billions are spent on cosmetic surgery, diets, beer commercials and beauty contests—all with the same message. You're not having fun, you're not normal, until you can fit into this ideal mold—and buy our products. It's a condition that psychologists call the Lake Wobegon Effect. It's related to an American radio program about a fictional town called Lake Wobegon. A place where "all the women are strong, all the men are handsome, and all the children are above average." There's no such place. There never will be. More than anything else, the world needs to rediscover what's normal. Disability is a normal part of being human. People with disabilities are ordinary people. This is not a form of denial. It is a fundamental recognition of our undeniable worth and our inseparable membership in the human race. Yet women with disabilities, especially, are often devalued by the institutions they should be able to count on most—their families and the women's movement. One feminist activist said, "Why study women with disabilities? They reinforce traditional stereotypes of women being dependent, passive and needy." To that I ask, who is an accomplice to that image? Who is abandoning the universal ideals of freedom and dignity in exchange for the easy path of appeasement? Appeasement has been defined as feeding your friends to the alligators in hopes that he'll eat you last. Everyone loses with that strategy. We must be flexible in its strategies, but we must stay honest to our cause.

The next lesson comes from Captain Picard, who said that one of the most important things in a person's life is to feel useful. This kind of usefulness implies more than identity. It's the source of pleasure for so much of life. As the character Alexis in *Deep Space Nine* once said, "We all work for our supper." You'll be surprised how much sweeter it tastes when you do.

Unfortunately, a majority of people with disabilities don't have the chance to taste the sweet rewards of work. Unfortunately, its usually stereotypes, not physical barriers that stand in the way. And these prejudices can come from the most troubling of sources.

I contracted polio when I was two years old. I don't remember it. But I do remember my parents telling me about the advice the doctor gave when it was time for me to leave the hospital. He told them, "Just put her in bed, she's going to be staying there the rest of her life." I had a college counselor who advised me that going after more education might hurt me. He warned that it was hard enough for a woman with a disability to get married; a master's degree would only intimidate a man more.

And I remember when I went after my first job as a secretary. The boss nearly didn't hire me because he worried that I couldn't carry coffee to him every morning. Talk about a double barrel insult— being doubted whether you could do something that you really shouldn't have to do in the first place! I should have been more assertive. But I was newly married and getting that first job was important to me. I did get the job. I'm embarrassed to admit that I actually practiced carrying the coffee. And I never spilled coffee on the boss's lap, although the temptation was real. These were all well-meaning professionals who believed that they knew what was best for me. But my life would be much different, and I probably wouldn't be with you today, if I had stayed within the boundaries of their expectations.

We are all unique. Each one of us has special gifts to add to the tapestry we call community. But I have been among those rehabilitation counselors and administrators who have shortchanged client dreams in the name of risk management.

If a person with a severe disability says they want to become a doctor, should I dismiss their dreams as fantasy? Dreams are important. They reflect deeply held values. Even if the dreams seem far beyond reach, they deserve to be explored. And with a little work, they can show the path to a person's giftedness, and how they can make a difference in the world. But too often, people in our business are afraid to risk client failures. We want to shelter them from defeat. And we're afraid that their failure at a job or an educational goal will be seen as a black mark against the system that tried to help. Yet as Rabbi Harold Kushner once said, pain is an unavoidable part of a normal life. Risk-taking and failures are normal for both individuals and organizations.

The next lesson comes from the powerful Klingon, Lt. Commander Worf, who after tasting prune juice for the first time, declared it a warrior's drink. Sometimes we need a new perspective to see familiar things as they really are. That's why this conference is so important. It brings together people with disabilities and families and professionals and advocates under one roof.

TASH may be the only professional association dedicated to people with severe disabilities, but its organization of nearly 9,000 members reaches beyond the professional ranks. And that's so important! Years ago, there was a bill in our state legislature to increase wages for personal attendants, so that high turnover rates could be reduced. Many prominent rehabilitation professionals came to the legislative hearings in support of the bill. But it was one consumer, named Terry Gutterman, who made the issue understandable to legislators by simply asking them to "Imagine giving the keys to your house to 14 different people in a single year." That message got through—I believe—in large part because of one small action by one person. The bill passed. In a September 8th speech, President Clinton relied on a similar story to bring home the urgent message that the pending work incentive improvement act must be passed, before many people with disabilities can afford to work. Clinton described meeting a man in New Hampshire who, if he had to pay his own health bills, would have had bills of $40,000 a year, and he desperately wanted to take a $28,000 job. President Clinton called the old system foolish, and then asked, "Wouldn't you rather have the man making $28,000 and giving some of it back in taxes as a productive citizen?" Groups and individuals have made a difference. And I believe with all my heart that it can happen again.

There's another reason why this conference is so important. And it can be summed up in Captain Picard's admonition that "Things are only impossible, until they're not."

I remember what my father said to me when I was in the second grade. He loved me very much. He wanted me to be prepared for the future. So he warned me that I would probably never get married. He told me that I should become a clinical psychologist. I eventually did. Then he said that I should work to be the best, so that I could be independent, because some day there might not be anybody around to take care of me. Hard words for a seven-year-old girl to hear. But my father loved me. And he wanted me to be prepared. What a difference it would have made, for myself and my parents, if there was a family next door where the mother also wore braces. A role model. A person with a disability who was married, who raised children, who was a nurturing and independent in her own right. Maybe even a corporate leader.

Professionals aren't the only ones who need to know that those labels can also belong to a person with a disability. People with disabilities need that affirmation, as well. The truth is, most boundary-breaking work has been done by people with disabilities who had the courage to challenge the status quo. Now we are facing the greatest challenges in the past 25 years. Last Spring's Olmstead decision bought us a temporary victory in the courts to protect the Americans with Disabilities Act, but the Florida Assistant Attorney General is now challenging the constitutionality of the ADA. The same backlash is being felt on the Individuals with Disabilities Education Act front.

> *What a difference it would have made, for myself and my parents, if there was a family next door where the mother also wore braces. A role model.*

Meanwhile, the waiting lists for services people with disabilities are entitled to are effectively creating their own blockades. Bureaucratic Quality Assurance systems are bogging down our service deliveries. We need to find ways to get monies to self advocates. We need to support vouchers for people with disabilities, so that they have choices about where to go for services. We need to have a Medicaid buy-in, so people can afford to go to work. And we need to provide more leadership opportunities for people with disabilities and self advocates.

At a time when college football stars are pleading guilty to illegally using handicapped parking permits and at a time when schools are refusing to pay for assistive technology, but buy elaborate lab equipment that only a few students will ever use and at a time when our most basic rights are being systematically attacked as too costly in an era of national prosperity—then its time for us to say enough with the abuse, the preferential treatment of the elite, and the pleading of poverty at a time of budget surpluses. Its time for us to say that Social Security Insurance is not the next and final step after high school graduation.

If detractors say we can't afford to do the right thing now, how long will it be before they say the time is right?

That brings us to the final lesson from *Star Trek*. I'd like to leave you with two quotations from Captain Picard that define what it means to be human.

In *The Next Generation*, Picard confronts discrimination by agreeing that, yes, we may be in different in appearance. Then he adds, "But we are both living beings. We are born, we grow, we live, and we die. In all the ways that matter, we are alike."

Then, later in the movie *Generations,* Picard confesses that "Recently, I've become very much aware that there are fewer days ahead than there are behind. But I took some comfort from the fact that the family would go on."

Much of what we do in the next two days will center on these fundamental beliefs: that we are alike, and that no matter who we are, we only have only a short time to accomplish what we desire to do.

Will our action steps create the world we want? No.

But they will bring that world closer. And the swifter we act, the more days of opportunities will be given to people with disabilities, and the fuller our own accomplishments will be. And for as long as it takes to reach our goal, there will be people like you and me, who will share that same vision.

I'm proud that you, and I, belong to that family.

IV. Health Care

American Medicine[1]

Moving from Practice to Business

Floyd D. Loop

M.D. and Chief Executive Officer, The Cleveland Clinic Foundation; the only surgeon serving on the 17-member Medicare Payment Advisory Commission, the panel that makes recommendations to Congress on Medicare policy; at the Cleveland Clinic, refined operative techniques for bypass surgery, 1971, and helped establish the world's first cardiovascular information registry, 1972.

Editors' introduction: Dr. Floyd D. Loop addressed the Standard & Poors Annual Healthcare Symposium at the Rancho Bernardo Inn Conference Center. With more than 200 persons from the financial community, Wall Street analysts, not-for-profit hospital executives, and managed care executives, he explored "the best and most attractive delivery system for patients, payors, purchasers, and physicians." Any "attempt to change health policy," Mr. Loop insists, "should not blunt . . . free choice, pluralism, diversity, independence, and privacy, and it should emphasize wherever possible, individual responsibility."

Floyd D. Loop's speech: When Winston Churchill entered the British Army as a commissioned officer in 1897, he was a picture of the Victorian colonial wars: cavalry boots, jodhpurs, pressed military tunic and choker collar. He was assigned to India and had to travel forty miles across a scorching plain and then up a steep winding road to Malakand Pass. He arrived disheveled, covered with yellow dust, and was then issued a tent, a seat at the staff mess, and a tumbler to be used for whiskey. This presented a problem for him because even at an early age, Winston Churchill had long enjoyed the taste of wine and brandy. The smokey taste of whiskey turned his stomach. However, here in the barrens, he faced a choice of tepid water, tepid water with lime juice, and tepid water with whiskey. As he put it, he "grasped the larger hope."

And, that's what I'm going to talk about: grasping the larger hope . . . first by a background of health policy and its ramifications; the financial realties of medicine today; the principles of a successful medical enterprise; and the concept of health care as an economic investment. How can medical organizations in an imper-

---

1. Delivered to the Standard & Poors Healthcare Seminar, San Diego, California, May 9, 2000. Reprinted with permission of Floyd D. Loop.

fect world, grasp this larger hope, and build the best and most attractive delivery system for patients, payors, purchasers, and physicians?

Factors Affecting Medicine

Medicine may be viewed as a product of four related factors. They are 1) demographics and trends, 2) healthcare policy, 3) payment and, 4) clinical practice. These variables cascade down upon one another, and ultimately affect the clinical practice of medicine. Each event has the potential for causing counter-reactions and triggering unintended consequence.

Demographics and trends are at the top of the cascade. The public-at-large is the driving force in health care and some of this activity is an index of the general economy. Here are a few examples of these demographic changes: of those born between 1946 and 1964, the first wave of seniors will arrive in 2010, and by 2030 more than 20% of the population will be 65 or older.

How can medical organizations in an imperfect world . . . build the best and most attractive delivery system for patients, payors, purchasers, and physicians?

There is a gradual shift in the ratio of workers to retirees, which will compromise future funding of retirement benefits. Today, there are 4 workers to every retiree; in 2020, it will be three workers for every retiree; and by 2030, the ratio will be two to one.

Other trends include ethnic shifts. In two decades, it is estimated that 22% of American children will be of Hispanic descent. The nature of labor is also changing. It has already transitioned from a larger capital base to smaller labor-intensive, more pan-time, temporary and contracted employment, rapid job turnover, and now a high probability of change in the financing of employer-based insurance.

These events affect health care policy. Congress knows that they have to control price and utilization. Unfortunately, many policies have an unintended effect of penalizing creativity, productivity, efficiency, and profit in health care. In Congress, they forgot that expanding benefits will not control spending. As Eugene McCarthy said, "the only thing that saves us from bureaucracy is its inefficiency."

Failure to control expenditures lead to government regulations. Failed government regulation leads to more government regulations, many of which add cost. The plural of anecdote is policy. It's interesting that at the time of the French revolution, the term liberal, as applied to economics and politics, meant free economy and minimal government. Something happened on the way through the past two hundred years.

The next rung down is payment. We know that physician payments are increasingly tied to the GDP; private payors not only follow government pricing, but also reduce their payments through authorizations, delays, and denials; we are operating more and more under price controls; and, the effect of tighter money is payment slowdown to physicians and hospitals.

All of these factors affect the clinical practice of medicine. The image of the solo practitioner whose armamentarium fit into a black bag is nostalgic, but clinical practice has evolved today into a complicated business, internally fractious, highly regulated, and subject to growing debate. The following trends have occurred in the past few years: the physician practice management industry is largely bankrupt; cost-saving in managed care is essentially exhausted; there is disunity among physician groups or societies; applications to medical school are down; and, the primary care specialty is no longer growing. It is abundantly clear that medicine is no longer a wealth building profession.

Let's look at the consequences. The effect of decreased payments on practice means declining service. The eventual impact of provider price controls will be to reduce time spent with patients, cutting amenities, limiting access, not updating equipment, and this generation of physicians is more likely to retire early. An example of policies affecting payment is exemplified by the federal Balanced Budget Act of 1997, which has harmed the hospital industry, especially academic medical centers, many of whom are now living on endowments. It has resulted in many hospital closures (although how many is not known, since such data is not collected in any standardized way).

The irony is that these policies have the effect of harming the very people they were intended to help. One good example of unintended consequences is the early result of lower payment on post-acute care, i.e., nursing homes, home health care, and rehabilitation. New government data shows that Medicare spending on home health dropped 45% in the past two years. Medicare payments for home health care will be automatically cut another 15% next year, unless Congress steps in to change it. Access for seniors will eventually be compromised. The economy today and our budget policies cannot accommodate tomorrow's retirement boom.

Generational accounting also offers a bad prognosis for the Medicare beneficiary. The longer the government waits to administer a change, the harder it will be on future beneficiaries. Today, a third of Medicare recipients have employer-sponsored coverage, but future retirees can't rely on subsidized employer-sponsored coverage to supplement Medicare. There has to be a new paradigm for funding Medicare so that people fund their retirement health care, perhaps through IRAs during their working years, and the government provides the supplemental payment . . . including protection for catastrophic illness.

Health Care Policy

Before we get into medicine and management, I want to review the road that government regulation is taking us down. These regulations, disguised as public interest, are a step-wise movement to government-run health care. In many instances, the unintended effect is to actually increase the cost of medicine.

The biggest federal intervention so far is the Balanced Budget Act which affects all sectors of medicine: hospital, ambulatory, and post-acute care. Next in order is the Health Insurance Portability and Accountability Act (HIPAA), which expands children's benefits, fraud and abuse investigations, and adds the privacy and confidentiality ruling (the privacy part is not yet final). It gives the patient the right to edit their record and de-identify data, and the provider has to document that the record was accessed outside care. It mandates a physician of record, and enforces security enhancements with criminal law. The government would prefer a federally controlled, universal patient medical base with unique patient identifiers, but even that is a bit of a stretch. The third federal intervention is the Patient's Bill of Rights, whose passage could effect employer-sponsored health care. The fourth intervention is the Medicare prescription drug benefits, which are likely to pass in some form. Incidentally, the U.S. is the only country in the world that has a free market for pharmaceuticals—something that must be a powerful incentive to the regulators. The fifth intervention is the mandatory reporting of medical errors; we anticipate the passage of some legislation in this area. Finally, there are the miscellaneous interventions, such as attempts to expand Medicare through a buy-in for ages 55-64; HCFA modernization—which is not all bad if it eliminates the two year data lag; more whistleblower suits; and the Emergency Medical Treatment and Active Labor Act (EMTALA), an antidumping provision that carries criminal penalties. The point is that we are moving step by step down the road to government-run health care.

Some people believe that government-run health care would be simpler and less expensive—in fact, many doctors are of that opinion. However, remember what Ronald Reagan said, "When you go to bed with the government, you better expect more than a good night sleep." The fact of the matter is that in our culture, a government-run system would ultimately be more expensive than the pluralistic approach we have today. For those who encourage the adoption of universal health care, ask them what will happen to 1) overall quality; 2) to access; 3) to students going into medicine; 4) what happens when you treat professionals as employees; and 5) the effect of generalists substituting for specialists. These are not theoretical concerns because they have occurred in several countries to the detriment of health care.

In our culture, a government-run system would ultimately be more expensive than the pluralistic approach we have today.

In non-medical for-profit businesses, expansion, development, and creation of values are celebrated. In the government financing of health care, improved performance, efficiencies, better result— all the things that create value—are often treated as punitive and are reasons to reduce reimbursement further.

Beyond basic care, every socialized medical system in the world has run into trouble. Even if the government could control cost by excessive rationing, regulating medical fees, limiting access, and controlling technology, the effect would be to reduce the innovation in science and ultimately retard the medical advances that will change our lifestyle even further. As economist Elizabeth Teisberg wrote, "Innovation is the only long-term solution to high-quality affordable health care."

In countries with universal systems, poor access is tolerated because the populations have different expectations. Nationalizing health care does not stop cost from rising, nor is it going to diminish public expectations. The advances in medicine that we enjoy today come from the burgeoning scientific research, entrepreneurialism, and excellent medical education. Yet, no other profession in our free market economy is subjected to anything like the imperious intrusion of the government into medical decisions and physician income.

Also, universal coverage doesn't make anyone healthier. Life expectancy varies across occupations and socioeconomic groups. The single greatest determinant of health status is education. Its been pointed out recently that in Canada and Germany, physicians have become like hamsters on a wheel of discounted fee-for-service and they are paid less and less for their time. It is very difficult to absorb all the new scientific advances and expect people to benefit optimally under hamster care. Universal health care is certainly not regulatory relief; it won't make the doctors any better off.

Canada was the sweetheart of health care a few years ago, but you don't read about it very much, now. A large number of efficiencies attributed to Canadian medicine are accounting artifacts. Health care worker benefits, cost of medical research and development, working capital, and operating costs of medical facilities are not recorded in Canadian health care expenditures. Also, they don't have the extent of problems that we medicalize, e.g., violence, drugs, AIDS, and teenage pregnancy.

The point is that the net effect of increased regulation could result in less employer-sponsored health care, less incentive to purchase insurance, higher price for those who purchase private coverage, more uninsured, and eventually more credence to those who say the system is inept and the government is better suited to regulate health care.

There is a limit to government solutions for all of our ills. In the past, we have been reminded that we tax work, investment, employment savings, and productivity, and we subsidize nonwork, consumption, and debt. Any program that assures that everyone will have health insurance will greatly affect the cost of insurance for people who already have coverage. Employers don't pay for health care, individuals do. Every dollar comes from private households. No system is perfect, but competition is better than all the known alternatives. Our pluralistic system protects and promotes advances in medicine, which benefit an increasingly expectant and informed humanity.

If these are the problems, what are the potential solutions? I would focus on three areas: 1) insure needed children—annual cost of about $1,000/child—already helped by the Federal/State Children's Health Insurance Program—the incremental cost to finish the job is estimated to be about $11 billion a year; 2) initiate catastrophic care insurance—no one should face financial ruin for an acute illness—mandatory for those who buy insurance and subsidized for those that are disadvantaged; 3) cap the tax benefit for employer-based health insurance. The American Medical Association favors a tax credit inversely related to income. The federal government could offer $75 to $100 billion in tax credit (current tax liability), which theoretically should induce people to purchase health insurance and reduce the amount of uncompensated care. The employers would have to shift programs from defined benefits to defined contributions; 4) What won't work? Throwing money at the uninsured—they are not a monolithic group—up to half of the uninsured could afford insurance, but it's not a priority for them; they're either too young or think they're too healthy and they would rather spend their money elsewhere. Policies should be aimed at encouraging people to be insured.

Medical Reimbursement

There are some interesting changes in health care payments with respect to costs. We'll use the figures from 1998 as an example, simply because those are the most recent available. Medicare/Medicaid payment-to-cost was at a low point ten years ago, but it was subsidized on the private side by inflated prices. However, the hydraulics have changed; payment-to-cost ratios on the private side have been falling since 1992. In the past 10 years, the ratio of private payments-to-cost dropped from about 1.30 to 1.14. The hydraulics of subsidizing low government payment by inflated prices on the private side is disappearing, however, Medicare payment to cost has improved, and by 1998, Medicare paid slightly more than $1.02 for every dollar expended by providers delivering care to beneficiaries. Remember that these trends have occurred in the face of dramatic decreases in cost throughout the hospital industry. Some have concluded that the plight of hospitals today is related to the falling payment/cost ratio on the private side.

Whereas, the government has effectively controlled prices, private side premiums are still negotiable. Health care premiums will increase 6-10% this year according to a survey of 600 companies and it may go up by a similar amount in 2001. Price drives cost, but the majority of excessive cost has been eliminated from clinical care. Already, hospitals have compensated for BBA by tighter controls, divestitures of unprofitable businesses, employee reductions, renegotiation of private contracts, dropping risk contracts, and outsourcing services.

The problem is that medicine is a service industry and our health care costs are higher in the United States, probably because of greater technology, higher productivity, and higher worker wages. Other countries pay their health professionals less—doctors, nurses, and technologists—and in general, they don't work at the same pace as we do in the United States. Knowledge, experience, improved technology, and pharmaceutical advances indisputably mean that patients are getting better care for their money even in the past two decades. While medical prices are rising, this is not due to declining competitiveness in the medical care market or to any ability of the physicians to extract higher fees. As the market is affected more and more by price controls, and regulations beget regulations, there will be less cooperation on the part of physicians as their incomes fail to compensate for rising costs. Eventually, qualified people will think twice about a medical career . . . and it may be happening already.

Average hospital or inpatient Medicare margins have dropped from 17% in 1997 to 13.1% in 1999 nationwide and are expected to fall to 11% soon. The nation's smaller hospitals are in greatest jeopardy.

It is interesting to review the net additive effect of the Medicare payments on total Medicare margin for a large integrated medical center. If one takes net income from inpatient activity, including graduate medical education, the hospital had a 25% margin of profit over expenses in 1999. In-patient revenue accounts for approximately 50% of the aggregate payments. In this case, in-patient revenues include monies for graduate medical education. Many academic health centers are not reimbursed for faculty teaching time or for support activities that relate to medical education. The

---

As the market is affected more and more by price controls, and regulations beget regulations, there will be less cooperation on the part of physicians.

---

added cost of graduate medical education has to be made up from other sources. Next, when we add Medicare reimbursement for outpatient activity, profitability falls substantially. The further addition of post-acute activities (like rehabilitation, skilled nursing, and home health care) the profitability decreases again. Adding professional reimbursement (physician fees) the aggregate Medicare margin drops to near zero. Finally, if you add risk contracts (capitation) to these components, Medicare becomes a loss, and depending on the percent of capitated business, this loss can be substantial. It's no wonder that Medicare risk contracts are considered a credit negative. None of these calculations take into context the growing amount of charity and uncompensated care rendered each year.

The Medicare Part A trust fund is reported to remain solvent until 2023, eight years longer than originally projected. The reason is that the 2.9% Medicare tax is applied today to a large payroll base, which has increased the Part A trust fund revenues by 19% in the past two years. We also have a sound economy today, a large number of workers per beneficiary, and low unemployment. There are two other factors that have improved solvency: 1) the BBA shifted payment for home health services from Part A to Part B, which immediately lengthened the viability of Medicare Part A from 2001 to 2007, and 2) processing delays by the government reduces the Medicare outlays by up to 2% annually.

Clinical Practice

Medicine requires a tremendous personal investment in training with less and less monetary return on that investment. The problems in medicine, apart from cost, may be attributed to individual practice, physician organization, and duplication of services.

In the area of individual practice, variation in diagnosis and treatment is widespread. Medicine is an imperfect science and is practiced by an estimate of probabilities and good clinical judgment based on experience. Our culture demands that high level technology is applied at the end of a natural life span. There are elements of absurdity in this practice, i.e., because something can be done—so something must be done. There are no uniform standards for quality measurement, which is difficult to measure because of the heterogeneity of patients and diseases. There are recertification requirements in medical specialties, but competence testing is lacking. This should be remedied as computer-based examinations are implemented.

There are flaws in the way medicine is organized in the United States. Specialty care is not regionalized—witness 150 heart transplant facilities. Also, there is lack of alignment between physicians and hospitals (with physicians having no input), acquisition of practices, which is not integration; and now, unionism which arises out of frustration from all of the above.

Physicians may not be riding first class today, but despite all the pessimism, I don't believe we are on the Titanic. The medical profession provides a vantage point from which physicians can see and even participate in change, participate in scientific discovery, and in accelerating progress. If that weren't enough, we actually help people. Medicine is part of real humanism that has few equals.

The Business of Medicine

Let's look next at the medical enterprise. Somewhere between investment and performance of the organization are the components related to the business of medicine: management, finance, delivery, and intangibles. Health care should borrow four principles from business: 1) any complex organization is best managed on a decentralized basis; 2) you need to hire the best people at every level; if you hire mediocre people, they will hire mediocre people; 3) focus on potential, not problems; 4) never hire anybody in a supervisory capacity who couldn't do the job of those they manage.

The strategy should be to invest in physicians and their leadership. This is the intellectual capital where value in medicine resides. Value in medicine is far more important than money. You can't put a price on hope, wisdom, skill, and compassion. Physicians are the talent in medicine, but they have an immature, unbridled desire for unmanaged freedom. Adam Smith pointed out that the only dependable human motive is self interest, but self-interest can be managed by aligning personal incentives with the organization. The object is to motivate the motivators; fame is what you take, character is what you give back. At the end of the day, the effectiveness of leadership is how well the individual physician understands the goals and performance of the organization and whether the clinical interdependencies create innovations that result in consistently better outcomes.

> *Value in medicine is far more important than money. You can't put a price on hope, wisdom, skill, and compassion.*

There are three reasons why leadership is critical in medicine: 1) we are beginning an era of physician-directed health care; 2) medicine is the business of results which demands leadership for database formation, benchmarking, and translation of knowledge into clinical application; and, 3) to assure that medicine doesn't devolve into a commodity that stifles innovation.

In medical center management, the purposes of profitability are to keep the mission intact, to provide workforce security, to invest for progress, and to pay off the debt. The main financial drivers are profitability, asset productivity, and capital structure. Financial performance depends to a great extent on success in asset management, i.e., deployment of technology and human capital that correlates with a good return on investment and at the same time, serves legitimate medical needs. This is a peculiar time; the brokers, the moneychangers, and the payors are in charge—not the provider or receiver of health care. This is an incredible phenomenon. There is no parallel in law, architecture, the arts, or other professions, or even in most industries. Commercialism in medicine is relentless and if it persists, it will erode the trust between the physician and patients, and economics will drive ethics even more than it does today. Although profit in health care is essential to provide services, running a strictly profit-maximizing corporation is different from a medical operation whose first priority is an obligation to the patient, science, and education. Money is necessary for success, but not the primary reason for the enterprise.

When Henry Ford started his own company, he reflected on what he first learned about business: "Thinking first of money instead of work brings on a fear of failure," he observed, "and, this blocks every avenue and makes man either afraid of his competition or afraid to change his methods. Yet the way is clear for anyone who thinks first of service—of doing the work in the best possible way.

On the deliverable side, multi-hospital systems don't have a good record of keeping promises or having demonstrable competitive advantage. However, there are exceptions. We were one of the first systems (we own 10 hospitals) that received Joint Commission System Accreditation largely because we showed the extent to which key support functions could be coordinated across operating units in the system. Market leadership also requires physician input at the community level and continuing education about cost, service, and outcome. To be successful, the parent organization must realize that patients want to stay in their own communities for health care. One of the biggest mistakes, of course, for any medical center is the acquisition of physician practices, which we avoided . . , money can't buy friends, all it does is give you a better class of enemies. Intangibles correlate with the reputation of the organization. The singular purpose of a medical organization is to benefit humanity through the efficient, effective, and ethical practice of medicine; to maintain the highest standards of quality; to honor creativity and innovation. Each member of the organization is a guardian of the enterprise and is responsible for assuring that the medical center is synonymous with the finest health care in the world. Physicians can live by that credo if they are aligned with the medical center. Differentiation occurs through their innovations. Name recognition, research and development, brand equity, the capacity for continued innovation, new successful programs, human resources (labor relations), and physician management are intangible factors that affect reputation. In short, intangibles means the level of success in creating social capital from investment capital.

Finally, I want to mention health care as an economic investment. The chief priorities of a developed nation are security, education, and health care. Health care will be around as long as we live. American health care has never been better if we can afford it. The challenge is how to make it affordable without ruining the value of modern medicine, which is founded on the benefits from science and education.

Earlier this year, England's health secretary, Alan Milburn, spoke at the London School of Economics and argued that health care spending is as much an economic as a social investment. He said that it's time to challenge conventional thinking that health spending is a debit, not a credit. Health care spending should be seen as an investment that builds economic infrastructure. In order to treat health care that way, he proposed that spending must meet two conditions: 1) an efficient organization of health care services that doesn't place an undue burden on the economy, and 2) that health care constitutes a preventive, as well as a sickness service.

I read an article in the *Economist* last year criticizing the United States. The essayist noted that while we dominate commerce, communication and military strength, we are inappropriately isolationistic when it comes to many of the world's problems. The writer thought that America should be like any other nation and behave the same way. Later, a fellow from California responded in a letter pointing out that "America is not a nation like any other, which is exactly why it leads the world. The U.S. is the only nation in the world not founded on nationality, not on ethnicity, not on tribalism, not on religion, but on ideas—the concepts of personal and economic freedom, liberty, and human rights."

These principles are as relevant today as they were at the time of our nation's founding. These enduring qualities have made us a beacon for the world in times of wellness and illness and, have produced a society here like no other. A challenge for our elected representatives is how to strengthen and live by these founding principles in the 21st century. Policymakers have to recognize that people eventually pay for all costs of medicine. Attempt to change health policy should not blunt the free choice, pluralism, diversity, independence, and privacy, and it should emphasize wherever possible, individual responsibility. As Thomas Jefferson said, "no more good must be attempted than the people can bear."

The Health Care Question and Market Solutions[2]

Raymond V. Gilmartin

President, chief executive officer, and chairman of the board, Merck & Co., Inc., 1994– ; born March 6, 1941; B.S., electrical engineering, Union College, 1963; MBA, Harvard Business School, 1968; vice president and later chairman, president, and chief executive officer of Becton Dickinson and Company, 1976–94; chairman of Healthcare Institute of New Jersey, and past chairman of the Pharmaceutical Research & Manufacturers of America, presently serving on its executive committee; trustee of the Healthcare Leadership Council and of Valley Health System, Inc.; chairman of the Council on Competitiveness and the board of associates of the Harvard Business School; a director of The College Fund/UNCF, and a member of the Business Roundtable and the Business Council.

Editors' introduction: President Gilmartin defined for the Economic Club of Detroit "the principles" which he believes "can responsibly improve quality and access in health care in a cost-effective way," those being "competition and choice."

Raymond V. Gilmartin's speech: It's a pleasure to be here today at the Economic Club of Detroit. My predecessor at Merck, Dr. Roy Vagelos, joined this group in the election season of 1992 to talk about the topic of the day, health care reform. For better and for worse, neither what was feared nor what was hoped for has come to pass, and once again, reform is on the national agenda. So let's make the topic a Merck tradition.

Seven years ago, candidate Bill Clinton was challenging the nation to dramatically change our health care system. Two years later, President Clinton's sweeping reform proposal failed just as dramatically, taking with it Democratic control of the House and Senate. Time passed, but the issue endured.

Today, companies large and small see health care as a key operating expense. Young people and baby boomers worry along with the elderly about health care costs and access to doctors of their choice. The deliberations of the National Bipartisan Commission on the Future of Medicare, which had initially planned to release its report today, have been widely covered in the news media—as

---

2. Delivered at the Economic Club of Detroit on March 1, 1999. Reprinted with permission of Raymond V. Gilmartin.

are a constant stream of stories of patients denied access to care. At this year's World Economic Forum in Davos, Switzerland, global leaders discussed health care investment, cost containment, and the pressures of aging populations in both developed and developing nations.

Against this backdrop of anxiety, our nation's progress in medicine, health education, and health infrastructure over the past half-century seems all the more remarkable. But our very progress underscores the challenges ahead. We live in the nation with the greatest medical care in the world. Yet 43 million Americans are uninsured. The U.S. virtually guarantees access to costly crisis and catastrophic care. Yet without guaranteed primary and preventive care, we guarantee an inefficient system.

Perhaps our greatest challenge is the all-too-common opinion that health care problems are intractable. That cost containment means

---

The cornerstones of the free marketplace— competition and choice—provide the best way to remove inefficiencies, control costs, and improve quality in health care.

---

care containment. That more efficiency equals less access. Compounding this sense of unease, the voices of special interests sometimes seem louder than those speaking for the public interest. Various groups use statistics or slogans to discredit others or stir fears. So today, I will try to limit the use of statistics and focus on the principles that I believe can responsibly improve quality and access in health care in a cost-effective way.

Competition

How can we do this? The cornerstones of the free marketplace— competition and choice—provide the best way to remove inefficiencies, control costs, and improve quality in health care. Market-based reform is not about giving up on our social contract. It does not mean reducing access to care or resorting to rationing. It means allowing competition to create a more efficient and more accessible system.

Competition sparks innovation, creating powerful incentives for new, more effective, and more cost-effective medicines and treatments. It's a relatively new approach in health care, and it's being greeted with skepticism. Yet it works.

The free market stimulated the private sector in our nation to discover half of the world's new medicines in the past ten years. The influence of the market and competition helped dramatically slow national health spending, which grew at 4.8% in 1997, its lowest rate in over three and a half decades. Health spending as a share of GDP actually *fell* slightly from 13.6% in 1996 to 13.5% in 1997.

These events defy the conventional wisdom of the 80s and early 90s that the market wouldn't work in health care. It does. Certainly, the free-market system is not perfect. It's unforgiving of inefficiency and bad policy, as social and economic events the world over have taught us. It can be disruptive for industry, as the failure of several HMOs have made clear. But competition does work for the benefit of the consumer, driving out the ineffective and unproductive—and it will work in health care. The government model is failing—and not just with Medicare, which if left unchanged, will run out of money as early as 2008. In Canada and in Europe, waiting times for medical procedures can run over a year. In Japan, innovation languishes without market incentives.

Some believe that every possible efficiency has been wrung from the health care delivery system since the introduction of managed care—that in fact managed care sacrifices quality and access to save money and gains made in cost management are unsustainable. Critics point to the recent withdrawal of some HMOs from Medicare because of unexpected cost increases.

It's true that until recently, much of the savings in health care came from driving hard bargains with hospitals and physicians, by creating gates and gatekeepers for patients. But future, sustainable savings will come from better prevention and health promotion, better patient care, better management of disease conditions, better health outcomes—in short, from the transition from cost management to quality and health management. Just as we successfully changed our manufacturing processes in the 70s and 80s to meet the demands of the marketplace and increase productivity, we can change health care delivery, which, along with innovative technological and medical advances, can improve the cost effectiveness of our health care system and reduce the burden of disease.

How can such changes simultaneously improve quality and maintain cost efficiency? Let me give an example. I serve on the board of Valley Hospital, a 430-bed hospital in New Jersey, which is redesigning its health care delivery system around patient needs, rather than around departments or medical disciplines. Start-to-finish care—not by different departments, but by cross-functional teams—covers all patient needs from pre-admission education to rehabilitation and home care. Sound familiar? It's what many of us in business and even some areas of government have been doing: breaking down the silos, organizing around products or customers, and using teams to better serve consumers.

One patient at Valley related her experiences of two hip replacements several years apart in different hospitals, the second at Valley. In the first, she had general anesthesia; in the second, local anesthesia followed by patient-controlled pain relief, reflecting advances in technology. The first time, she was in the hospital 10 days. The second time, she was home in 3 days, where she completed most of her rehabilitation and physical therapy. Before she even arrived at the hospital, Valley personnel met with her at home and told her about the process, down to details like the dangers of throw rugs during rehabilitation. They gave her a video detailing what to expect. Overall, she recovered faster, had less pain, and received better care at dramatically less cost. She was less likely to suffer from infection because of the shorter hospital stay and less likely to fall because of education.

The new approach is not about shortcuts or drive-through surgeries. It's about practices that optimize around patients, serving them better and more effectively. It's working on a large scale at Valley, and patient satisfaction is high.

This example of process improvement is just one of many areas in which physicians and managed care organizations have sought to improve quality in recent years. Others include clinical practice guidelines and evidence-based medicine, pharmaceutical health management and efforts to reduce medication errors in hospitals, and quality measures based on patient preference leading to health plan report cards.

Evidence-based medicine lends objective criteria to decision making. Outcomes data can show that a product or procedure reduces the need for surgery, time in the hospital, or death rates and improves health and quality of life, thereby helping to deliver better care and better cost effectiveness. For example, a class of drugs called ACE inhibitors has been proven to reduce hospitalizations and mortality from congestive heart failure. Yet less than half who could benefit from these medications are being treated. Such knowledge can be used to manage resources more effectively and provide preventive care that can reduce the need for expensive emergency care or hospitalization.

Merck is committed to such strategies and to health management to deliver high-quality, cost-effective care that properly uses medicines with demonstrated value. For example, the government calculates that inappropriate prescription drug use costs the American health care system 20 billion dollars a year. Because seniors take one-third of all prescription drugs and face serious potential risk from dangerous drug interactions or from medications or dosages generally deemed inappropriate for the elderly, our Merck-Medco managed care subsidiary created "Partners for Healthy Aging." This program links physicians and pharmacists to provide a comprehensive view of a patient's prescription drug use, and *The Journal of the American Medical Association* recently published results *[October, 1998]* demonstrating the program's success in detecting and preventing inappropriate prescription drug use. Though the program focuses on safety and quality of care, it also saves money.

Health management programs that incorporate best practice guidelines and provider and patient education strategies can also help patients adhere to drug regimens, to improve quality of care and reduce expensive hospitalizations.

Information technology can be used to identify standards of care and best medical practices, as there are often wide variations of treatment of medical conditions—and hence excessive swings in outcomes and costs. [This is another concept we recognize from business. Pioneered at Western Electric in the 1920s, "statistical process control" identifies variations in a process and then narrows the variations to improve quality.]

Of course, other arenas for process improvement exist. Why, then, haven't all health care providers become as efficient as possible? A lesson can be drawn from the American corporation, a relatively recent organizational entity in the history of business, dating to the turn of the century. Then, new American corporate organizations faced difficulties and failure, leading some to believe that corporations were not a workable or even desirable organizational form. Yet with time, a cadre of professional managers helped develop one of the most effective organizational systems in history. Similarly, entrepreneurs and hospital management still face growing pains as they determine how best to efficiently and effectively provide care. Market forces, increased competition, and more informed consumers create management and professional challenges. Health plans are not the only ones affected: these same factors are changing the way doctors, hospitals, and pharmaceutical companies operate. Some of these entities may fail. Some may take the most basic cost-cutting actions. But the truly successful ones will take the kinds of steps I've talked about—and develop creative new ones—that work toward both increasing quality and cost-effectiveness.

Investment

I've spent a fair amount of time thus far talking about cost-effectiveness. I use this term rather than "cost" alone because it's important in this debate to explode the myth that we spend too much on health care. Too often, in both developed nations and those struggling to meet the basic needs of their citizens, those in the public and private sectors alike see resources allocated to health care as a cost, rather than as an investment. However, a healthy population is an essential element of economic growth and productivity—as essential as roads and power plants and education. Disease and chronic conditions drain productivity. The answer is not to invest less—in fact, it may be to invest *more*, and certainly more efficiently in order to maximize outcomes.

Rather than asking, "Are we spending too much on health care?" let's start to ask, "What is the economic and human return on every health care dollar invested?"

Investment in health care means supporting innovation in health care, to ensure the kind of continued medical success that distinguished the past half century. Government support of a free-market environment conducive to innovation is critical. So is an awareness that innovation may well increase costs in the short-term—but it is cost-*effective*.

> ### Rather than asking, "Are we spending too much on health care?" let's start to ask, "What is the economic and human return on every health care dollar invested?"

Seven years ago, Dr. Vagelos spoke of potential medicines to treat HIV and slow its progression. That year marked the discovery of indinavir sulfate, or *Crixivan*, a new protease inhibitor Merck was able to bring to market in record time. Thanks in part to this and other innovative medicines, AIDS mortality rates have dramatically declined in the U.S. and Europe. Reports today call HIV a chronic, manageable disease, which now can require fewer expensive hospitalizations. Just as innovations in telecommunications, technology, and software have increased quality while reducing price, innovation in medicine can alleviate the burden of disease, more effectively allocate resources, and improve the quality of life. Other breakthroughs in cancer and heart disease, osteoporosis and asthma are doing just that.

As a result of innovation, many Americans today receive the finest health care in the world. In the nation that discovered the polio vaccine and pioneered prenatal care—that daily moves closer to conquering cancer and diabetes—new technologies and medical advances prolong and improve lives.

I cannot discuss the success of our investments and innovation to date without noting that while there is a rising tide of prevention and cure in many parts of America, disease and premature death still sweep over others, particularly lower-income neighborhoods.

The lack of primary care coverage, access, and health promotion contributes to health problems from higher smoking rates to higher infant mortality rates.

What *hasn't* improved since 1992 is the problem of America's uninsured.

Today, millions of Americans are without access to decent primary care, but when a crisis hits and they show up at the emergency room, they aren't turned away, even if they can't pay. We do what a compassionate and sensible society must do. But we also pay. We pay millions to treat sickness and disease that could have been prevented or treated earlier for far less. When an elderly woman suffers a disabling hip fracture that could have been prevented through earlier detection of osteoporosis, she pays the human price. Our society pays the financial one.

When a child is debilitated by asthma that could have been diagnosed earlier and treated for a fraction of the cost and a fraction of the pain, that child pays the human price. Our society pays the financial one.

Uncompensated care accounts for a huge portion of spending. It's a hidden tax that makes our system more expensive, less efficient, and less effective. And over and over again, there is a terrible human price. The solution is not to make government the single payer for health care, when we have the best private system in the world, but to keep what works, and to fix what doesn't. Some say the real problem is that we've been afraid to ration health care, to draw the line on who is entitled to certain kinds of care. But we as a society do not want to ration care, and we won't have to, if we address the inefficiencies in the health care system by stimulating competition and choice.

Medicare

The changes I have discussed today—among them prevention and primary care, patient-centered care, health management, new technologies, and above all, a health care system designed around choice and competition—are entering the U.S. health care system. Yet one arena is left untouched. Medicare, which provides care to 39 million elderly and disabled persons—remains mired in a 1960s model of American health care.

In creating this program thirty-five years ago, our nation made a promise to the elderly. We pledged that no one would have to face the prospect of old age without adequate medical care. I believe that to maintain our original promise to our parents and grandparents, we must now modernize Medicare, for it has not taken advantage of the best private sector innovation I've mentioned today. There is little incentive to coordinate care around the patient, to focus on prevention, to rapidly adapt technology, or to practice the most basic principles of health management. Today's reimbursement rules in fact often reward inefficiency, favoring long hospital stays even when medical advances and patient preference make them unnecessary.

Further, as I'm sure you know, Medicare does not provide prescription drug coverage. *That* must change. Pharmaceuticals today are essential to health care for the elderly. Thirty-five years ago, few treatments existed for chronic disease for the elderly. Today, medications treat and prevent heart disease, osteoporosis, and countless other previously debilitating conditions, increasing the quality and length of life.

The pharmaceutical industry may have stood in the way of such coverage in the past. But today, the Pharmaceutical Research and Manufacturers of America (PhRMA) supports prescription drug coverage for the elderly, as long as competition and innovation are part of the system. As it stands, the current government-run system, like public sector systems in Europe and Japan, is economically unsustainable. Prescription drug coverage could add 20 to 40 billion dollars a year in costs if simply tacked on as a stand-alone benefit.

A new solution is necessary.

Merck supports providing prescription drug benefits to Medicare beneficiaries by way of a thorough modernization of the program. Just like the successful health plan models used by private employers and the federal government, which incorporate the principles of quality and competition, a reformed Medicare program would enable beneficiaries to select from a range of private health plans, provide information toward making informed choices among plans, fund an adequate financial contribution to pay for all or a portion of the chosen plan, and contain costs through marketplace competition, not government price controls.

A reformed Medicare program based on quality, real consumer choice, and competition will not only preserve and strengthen Medicare into the next century, but will help facilitate continued incentives for medical innovations, including the discovery and development of important new medicines.

I am encouraged that members of the Medicare commission, including its chairman, Senator John Breaux, as well as Congressman Bill Thomas, are thinking along the same lines of competition and choice. We look forward to the report and the debate it will trigger. This said, I am aware of the challenges to the type of change I am describing, including political pressures and entrenched constituencies. Fear and resistance to change will no doubt hamper the process. The Clinton health care reform proposal left some with deep suspicions of any kind of overhaul. Similarly, years of heated debate of the federal budget have left others with fear that the federal government will renege on its contract with the nation's elderly. And, not surprisingly, decades of pharmaceutical industry anxiety that Medicare's coverage of medicines would lead to government price controls have created skepticism that our particular industry indeed cares about the elderly and is open to change.

I can only tell you that Merck is fully committed to change along the lines I have discussed today—not just for Medicare but for health care systems around the world.

If a social and economic history of America tells us anything, it is that those who do not anticipate the changes ahead are left behind. Merck has always been in the forefront of innovation—in medical discovery and in health care system change—and we are determined to remain on the forefront.

In America, we have always had great faith in our medical and scientific prowess. We never stop believing in the potential for technological advancements, for better treatments, for cures, even in the face of setbacks and failure. We also have confidence in the future of corporate America, as the Dow-Jones and mutual funds and thousands of new start-ups tell us. Someday soon, I think we'll share this kind of conviction in the future of our health care system—that we will in the next century provide the best of medicine to the greatest number of people.

Taking Care of Health Care[3]

Preserving the Relationship between Physicians and Patient

Thomas R. Reardon

M.D. and member of the AMA's Board of Trustees, 1990– , and its Executive Committee, 1994– ; president, American Medical Association (AMA), 1999–2000; born in Delta, CO; M.D. from University of Colorado School of Medicine, 1959; U.S. Air Force, 1960–63; president, Multnomah County Medical Society in Oregon, 1980–81; president, Oregon Medical Association, 1983–84; Congressional Physician Payment Review Commission, 1986–94; President's Advisory Commission on consumer Protection and Quality in the Health Care Industry, 1997–98; current council member, National Forum for Health Care Quality Measurement and Reporting.

Editors' introduction: Dr. Thomas R. Reardon spoke in his hometown to members of the Portland City Club convened at the Multnomah Athletic Club in Portland, OR. Questioning whether "government and our business enterprise systems . . . understand what is best for everyone," Dr. Reardon argued that any health care proposal must first serve patients' needs, that physicians only have to determine "what is necessary to treat disease."

Thomas R. Reardon's speech: Thank you, Mr. Anderson. And thank you, ladies and gentlemen. It's an honor to represent the American Medical Association before this important and influential gathering. In the last several months, as president of the AMA, I've traveled all over this great country and overseas, as well.

Wherever I travel, when I say I'm from Portland, people want to know about this city and its people. They see Portland as a world-class city, and Oregon as a wonderful place to live, with an enviable climate both in terms of weather, and in terms of people and business.

Back in January, you heard in this forum from both the mayor and the governor about the State of the City and of the State of Oregon. They both spoke of making Portland and the Oregon even better places than they already are. And, quite appropriately, each of them outlined a series of programs and projects to do that.

---

3. Delivered to the Portland City Club, Multnomah Athletic Club, Portland, Oregon, May 26, 2000. Reprinted with permission of Thomas R. Reardon.

What struck me was an unspoken assumption in both addresses and in much of the news and public debate these days. And that is the unspoken assumption is that each of us will be healthy and active and able to do the work.

For Portland, for Oregon, indeed, for the United States, to be the best it can be means literally that each of us has to be the best we can be. And that begins with best of good health.

That unspoken assumption is one end of an interesting progression of thinking about health and the healthcare system in this country. At the other end of the spectrum is the unspoken assumption that the government and our business enterprise systems, together, understand what is best for everyone.

In point of fact, that assumption is just as open to question as the assumption that somehow good health is a "given." When you look at the health care issues today you find that they are very much on the minds of Americans. And very much at a critical decision-making point, as well.

For that reason, the AMA began last December to take the first steps into a new venture for us, which we called AMA's National House Call.

A venture some would say is quite audacious for the AMA.

We wrote a letter to each of the candidates for the White House, saying, and these are the words we used: "No candidate can be elected next November without a solid commitment to the issues that mean the most to patients."

And, for us, those issues are the ones that poll after poll tell us are on the minds of Americans. Those issues really revolve around three major concerns: health insurance company accountability, health coverage for all Americans and meaningful reform of Medicare.

Our goal was, and is, to bring those issues to the candidates. And we traveled to key primary states, putting the issues before all of the candidates.

Our goal was, and is, to bring those issues to the media. And we held press briefings and editorial discussions with newspaper and broadcast outlets all over the country.

Our goal was, and is, to bring the issues to the public. And we are finding voters all over America appreciate learning about the issues from a third party like the AMA.

We are convinced that an informed electorate is the bedrock on which democracy rests. AMA's National House Call is good, old-fashioned, local politics at its best. It's grassroots. It's populist in the best sense of that term. It's American as apple pie.

And we further believe that $100 million dollar propaganda campaigns, such as that one being conducted by the managed care insurance firms right now, are doomed to fail.

Not because advertising fails, but because grassroots activism succeeds.

The subject of that propaganda campaign, as you might expect, is the enormously popular, bipartisan Patients' Bill of Rights legislation in Washington. The House of Representatives passed the bill overwhelmingly after the AMA and others lobbied at the grassroots level for more than six years.

That lobbying, and the bill that resulted, focuses on an effective and fair Patients' Bill of Rights:

One that leaves to the physician the job of deciding what is necessary to treat disease, not an insurance company's procedures manual.

The AMA is committed . . . to protecting the rights of patients. It's not a Republican issue. It's not a Democratic issue. It's a patient issue.

One that creates an effective appeals process for patients whose care decisions by their physician are over-ruled by cost accountants and harm results.

One, further, that assigns responsibility and clearly establishes accountability in that process.

One that says, in effect, if you over-rule a physician's decision and harm results, you pay the consequences, Mr. Insurance Man.

We've taken that message to Congress. The House heard it and responded. Unfortunately, the Senate passed an insurance protection bill. And the two are in conference committee now, and the issue is in the balance.

What is not in question now, however, is the commitment and persistence of the AMA. If no positive action is taken in Washington before the end of this session of Congress we will take the issue into the November elections. And beyond November, if we have to.

The AMA is committed in no uncertain terms to protecting the rights of patients. It's not a Republican issue. It's not a Democratic issue. It's a patient issue.

In the same vein, the AMA is committed to healthcare coverage for all Americans. But, just as the National House Call is a first for the AMA, our approach to health care coverage for all Americans involves a new approach.

Late last year, the AMA convened a multiple-player conference, which we call, the Health Sector Assembly. It was a gathering of representatives from the whole spectrum of health care, from patient advocacy groups to government to managed care organizations, hospitals, think tanks, nursing organizations and every other group we could think of.

We met, not to gain consensus on some master plan for total solution to every problem. Rather, we met to carve out the broad outlines of the problems associated with coverage for all Americans. To agree on the nature of the problems to be solved. To find at least the level of willingness to provide a basic menu of coverage options. And some might be surprised at this but we actually found that willingness.

It was the old American spirit, if you will. It was the spirit of, "Let's roll up our sleeves and start to hammer out some answers."

And, most importantly, we agreed that, yes, the time is now. We can't evade our responsibilities for those 44 million men, women and children without adequate health care coverage today. We can't delay any longer.

Moreover, we said we need to define a basic level of coverage, and it could result in a two- or three-tiered approach.

But that, whatever the plan, we don't want to disturb the 85% of Americans already covered. And we need to take account of the fact that, of the 44 million uninsured today, fully four out of five of them are working Americans. They just don't have the employer-provided coverage, or the co-op payment plans of the rest of their working colleagues. They are in low paying jobs, or they just started a new job, or their household budget just won't stretch to cover health insurance after food, housing and other family expenses are covered.

The Patients' Bill of Rights the National House Call health care coverage for all Americans; these are some of the major issues. But one that looms even larger than these in my mind, is the disaster waiting to happen—a disaster we call Medicare.

The booming, $8 trillion dollar U.S. economy has been roaring along, generating enormous tax revenues. And the surpluses have sloshed into the so-called Medicare trust fund, giving added life to the projections for Medicare's fiscal future. But that economic engine may not roar along forever. And if it slows, if it stops masking the inequities and imbalances in the Medicare financial structure the hue and cry will be enormous.

The AMA has been asking for nearly a decade for meaningful reform. The clock is ticking. More than twice as many Americans will be eligible for Medicare 10 or 20 years from now as are eligible today.

When the claims come in and that trust fund runs dry, what then? We believe Medicare can be saved, can be redesigned, can be made so much more efficient so that the funds will be there with room to spare. But we need to raise Medicare on the agenda of public discussion.

These issues make for interesting conversation in the abstract. But we physicians have to deal with the consequences of them every day in the examining rooms and operating rooms and nursing homes of this country.

Let me tell you what I've seen in the last few weeks.

I met a family at a pediatric hospital in Des Moines, Iowa. One of the parents told me that their daughter needs medications that cost $5,000 a month. And their insurance requires a co-payment of 20%. Now, I don't have to do the math for you to have you figure out that that's $12,000 that family has to pay every year. Just for medications alone.

At an Iowa internist's office, I met a man who had quit his job to start his own business. But now he could not afford to buy health insurance as an individual.

Another man was in his 70s. And he was suffering from heart disease. His doctor had prescribed multiple medications. Now he's well past the age of retirement. So his wife has gone back to work just to pay for those pills.

And then, there was the story that still makes my blood run cold. A story I will never forget. Because I met another man that day. He had just turned 62. And he said to me, "Doctor, I lost my job to a younger man when I was 59. And I lost my health coverage.

"Now, I have a lung tumor. And I have to decide whether to spend my resources on radiation and chemotherapy to buy an extra year of life or to forego treatment now and leave something for my wife."

No one in the United States of America should ever have to make a decision like that. That man had a choice. Between selling his house to pay for treatment. Or leaving his wife with a roof to cover her head once he was gone. In the end, after long talks with his doctor and his wife, he decided to end his treatment, so that his wife would have a roof over her head.

I have concluded, and I know you will agree, that it is high time we put the "care" back into health care. And I believe, the AMA believes, the physicians of America need to take the lead.

For too long, now, physicians have been on the defensive, and I think wrongly so. For too long, now, physicians have been guilty of assuming somehow the politics and economics of medicine will take care of themselves. Well, they haven't and they won't.

But, physicians have a terrific story to tell, a story that will lead to solutions to our political and economic problems. And that story begins with just a brief reminder to the American people of how dramatic the improvements have been in health care over the last 75 or 80 years.

Before the 1920s, when insulin was discovered; before immunizations were developed; before the advent of antibiotics, of sulfa in the 1930s and penicillin in the 1940s.

Then we could finally, truly, cure—actually begin to treat disease. The acute and often fatal became the chronic and controllable. And the host of new technologies since that have doubled the life expectancy of Americans.

Now, with the advent of the human genome project, we will soon not only diagnose and treat. We will be able to predict and truly prevent disease.

Again, let me put that into human terms for you. Angina used to confine its victims to their homes. Arthritis doomed its victims to crutches or canes or wheelchairs. Cataracts meant blindness.

Now, I have angina patients whose angioplasty liberated them to a rich new life expectancy.

I have joint replacement patients who never think about crutches and canes but are traveling the globe with their friends.

And cataract patients whose lens replacement surgeries have them reading and looking at the sights without a care in the world.

All of this has a price. But that price should not be considered just in terms of cost or expense. It should be considered as an investment.

Not long ago, Senator Mark Hatfield asked some economists at the University of Chicago to evaluate that investment. They found that, every year, improved longevity in the health of Americans produced nearly $3 trillion added to the nation's gross domestic product of goods and services.

That's roughly one-third of our total G.D.P. And it's more than double the outlays for health care, the $1.2 or $1.3 trillion dollars the public sector and private sector spend in total. I can't think of many areas of the economy which cost half what they add to the bottom line.

And that's why I say, far from apologizing for its cost, we should rejoice in the improvements that our health care investment in infrastructure produce for us.

Every health care system in the world is in trouble. But where in the world do you go when you want the best medical care? The technology of medicine, the natural science of medicine, is exploding and creating new miracles every day and driving up costs in the process.

We physicians have a moral obligation to improve the quality of life. And our track record is very good. I believe we also have a moral obligation to point out three things:

First that medicine has increased the quantity of life expectancy;

Second that medicine has increased the quality of those added years;

Third, that our future lives, and the lives of our children and grandchildren, are directly tied to a health care system badly in need of reform, revision and correction.

Let me summarize the short-term outlook for medicine this way:

First, America's physicians will continue to advocate on behalf of their patients, all 274 million of them.

Second, America's physicians will be fighting for a healthcare system that covers all Americans, with a basic level of coverage and with programs that hold underwriters accountable for abusive practices and life-threatening meddling.

Third, America's physicians will be adapting and adopting the new information technologies, along with the medical technologies, that insure that this nation continues to receive the best medical care on earth.

I began by citing the two extremes in public perceptions of medicine, and used the example of our governor and your mayor, and the unspoken assumption of good health.

And I spoke of the equally prevalent assumption that healthcare issues were matters of costs and expense, rather than investment in the human infrastructure of the nation.

It's the wise investment in the infrastructure of this great nation. Now, America's health care is not a right it's a social obligation we ought to extend to everyone.

And finally, our health care system is not a second-rate system, else why do all the nations of the earth send their medical students here to learn? Or send their sick and dying here for treatment and cure?

And it's not perfect, but can be improved.

So, I conclude by saying the AMA is working hard to put the "care" back into healthcare. It cares for; it cares about, and will continue to care on a massive scale and with incredible success rates.

The AMA will continue to care as it has for 153 years, about advancing the state of the art, about upholding the highest ethical practices and standards in the world, about protecting and enhancing and preserving that miraculous relationship between patients and their physicians. Thank you.

Helping Women across the Arc of Life[4]

Donna E. Shalala

U.S. Secretary of Health and Human Services, 1993– ; born in Cleveland, OH, February 14, 1941; B.A., Western College for Women, 1962; U.S. Peace Corps, Iran, 1962–64; Ph.D., Maxwell School of Citizenship and Public Affairs, Syracuse University, 1970; taught political science at Bernard Baruch College, New York City, 1970–72; taught politics and education, Columbia Teacher's College, 1972–79; director and treasurer, Municipal Assistance Corporation, 1975–77; assistant secretary for policy research and development, Department of Housing and Urban Development (HUD), 1977–80; president of Hunter College, New York City, 1980–88; chancellor, University of Wisconsin–Madison, 1988–93; chaired the Children's Defense Fund, 1980–93; more than two dozen honorary degrees; National Public Service Ward, 1992; Glamour magazine's Woman of the Year, 1994.

Editors' introduction: Secretary Donna E. Shalala addressed the Women's Equality Summit on two related issues: child care and Medicare. Dr. Shalala praised the initiatives of the Clinton Administration on behalf of child care for "working families," but as "steps to build on—not to rest on." "For older women," the Secretary reminded, "Medicare isn't just a support system—it's a lifeline."

Donna E. Shalala's speech: When I was preparing my remarks for today, I recalled that near the end of her life, Gertrude Stein turned to Alice Toklas and said, "So what's the answer?" When Toklas didn't know, Stein turned to her again and slowly said, "In that case, what's the question?"

For this Administration—since day one—the question we've been trying to answer is how do we address the needs of every woman, every day, everywhere? As the First Lady and Secretary Herman discussed, we're working to do just that on a number of fronts. We've invested in women's education and training by providing Hope Scholarships, Lifetime Learning Tax Credits, and an increase in Pell Grants. We're helping working women care for their kids by extending health insurance to millions of children. And we've expanded women's economic opportunities by passing the Family & Medical Leave Act, extending the Earned Income Tax Credit, and raising the minimum wage. These are all great

4. Delivered at the Women's Equality Summit, Washington, D.C., March 15, 1999.

accomplishments for women. Accomplishments that also underscore this Administration's aim to help working families. And accomplishments to be proud of.

But today I want to focus on two specific priorities of ours—child care and Medicare. These two issues may seem completely unrelated. But they demonstrate our firm commitment to address the needs of women across the entire arc of life—From the young mother struggling to care for her children, to the elderly grandmother whose children may need to take care of her.

When it comes to addressing the needs of many working women, we have to start with child care. Because whenever I talk with working mothers—and fathers—who are struggling to balance the demands of work and family, the conversation inevitably turns to their child care concerns. That's why I'm proud of what this Administration has done for child care. We've helped states establish health and safety standards. We've promoted partnerships between child care and health care agencies. We've brought the public and private sectors together to offer more child care that families can depend on. And in 1997, the President and First Lady hosted the nation's very first White House child care conference.

We've done a lot to ease the child care concerns of millions of working families. But these are steps to build on, not to rest on. And we still have much to do. As the President said when he proclaimed March as "Women's History Month:" "We must promote policies and programs—including affordable, high quality child care—that enable working women to succeed both on the job and in their homes."

The President knows that child care needs a giant booster shot. And that's exactly why he proposed his Child Care Initiative—the largest single investment in child care in our nation's history. The initiative will help relieve what today's working parents always tell me are the three biggest child care headaches: Can I find it? Can I afford it? Can I trust it? It will help families find child care by creating more care, particularly after-school care for up to half a million children per year.

It will help families afford child care by doubling the number of children receiving child care subsidies. And by providing greater tax relief to help working parents pay for child care—or to support those parents who choose to stay at home and care for their children.

Finally, this initiative will help families trust child care by providing 3 billion dollars over 5 years to improve the quality of care to train providers and to help states enforce their own health and safety standards.

The President's initiative isn't only an investment in child care. It's an investment in America's working families. It's an investment in America's future. It's an investment in the possibility and potential of every child. And it will help ensure that no one will ever have to choose between being a good worker and a good parent. I'm glad to report that tomorrow, we expect representatives Cardin of Maryland and Tauscher of California to introduce comprehensive child care bills in Congress that reflect the President's initiative. Quality child care is a promise we need to keep for every working mother.

But, for those women who have already watched their children, and they're grandchildren, grow up for those women who are at the other end of life's arc, we have a very different promise to keep—the promise of Medicare.

The difference that this single program has made in the lives of our older Americans reminds me of a story about the famous writer, Somerset Maugham. Maugham was asked to address a group on his 80th birthday. When the author was introduced, he slowly rose. He thanked his hosts. He took a few sips from his glass of water. He then began by saying, "Old age has many benefits." And he suddenly stopped. Maugham looked around. He fidgeted. He sipped some more water. At last, he said dryly and slowly, "Old age has many benefits—I'm just trying to think of some."

Maugham, of course, was trying to be funny. But when he made that remark a half century ago, there was a sad ring of truth in his words. At the time, growing old meant poverty. Growing old meant disability. And growing old meant going without health insurance. As late as 1956, only 56% of America's seniors had insurance for hospital care. They often had to choose between saving their health or spending all they had saved. But when President Johnson signed Medicare into law, he changed what it meant to grow old in America. Today, Americans are living 20% longer, and the poverty rate among senior citizens has dropped in half since the 1960's.

Medicare promised the best health care in the world for older Americans. And for nearly 35 years, our nation has recognized that we must keep this promise—especially for our older women. Women have longer life spans than men. Elderly women are nearly twice as likely to be poor as other seniors. They comprise the majority of our nursing home population. They are more likely to suffer from a severe disability or have a crippling disease—like osteoporosis or arthritis—than elderly men. And nearly three-quarters of all Medicare beneficiaries over age 85 are women.

When it comes to addressing the needs of many working women, we have to start with child care.

For older women, Medicare isn't just a support system—it's a lifeline. From the very beginning, this Administration has worked to ensure that the lifeline isn't broken. That growing old in America is never again synonymous with poverty and disability. And that we keep the promise of Medicare not only for ourselves, but for our daughters and granddaughters. That's why we've extended the life of the Trust Fund for 10 years and formed a Bipartisan Commission to address Medicare's long-term challenges. That's why we've cracked down on Medicare fraud, waste and abuse, increasing the number of fraud convictions by 240%. That's why we've added new benefits—including mammograms, pap smears and bone density screenings—to prevent and detect diseases in women. And that's why we've made Medicare more efficient through market-oriented reforms—reforms such as new plan choices, prudent purchasing provisions and payment system improvements. All of these actions will help reform and transform Medicare into a more efficient and responsive program.

If we really want to keep the promise of Medicare for generations to come, to paraphrase the poet, we still have miles to go.

But if we really want to keep the promise of Medicare for generations to come, to paraphrase the poet, we still have miles to go. In fact, we face two paramount challenges—we must secure and strengthen the program.

Our first challenge is to secure Medicare. As I'm sure you're aware, President Clinton is proposing to use one in six dollars of the budget surplus for Medicare for the next 15 years. That will keep the Trust Fund solvent for two decades while we work out an even longer-term solution. And we have to do this now because the program is facing a demographic time bomb. As the President pointed out, the Baby Boom is about to become a Senior Boom, with the number of elderly Americans doubling by the year 2030. We must guarantee that Medicare will be there not only for the Baby Boom generation, but for generation "X," generation "Next," and every generation.

But it isn't enough to just secure Medicare; we must also strengthen the program. And that's our second challenge. We must make Medicare more competitive by adopting the best management, payment, clinical and competitive practices used by private industry. And we must guarantee a defined set of benefits without excessive new costs to beneficiaries.

We've also proposed that uninsured workers ages 62 to 65—and all other Americans ages 55 to 62 who have lost their jobs and health insurance through no fault of their own—be allowed to buy into Medicare.

To complement our Medicare reform efforts, the President has proposed the first long-term care strategy in our nation's history. The crux of our five year, six billion dollar initiative, is a targeted 1000 dollar long-term tax credit—paid for as part of our balanced budget—for people with long-term care needs or their caregivers. The initiative would also include an effort to inform all Medicare beneficiaries about long-term care options, since they may know very little about their choices.

Of course, when we discuss Medicare beneficiaries, we must ensure that the concerns and interests of women are not consigned to the backwater or the back burner. And that's where all of you come in. I'm reminded of a story involving the great Casey Stengel. When asked about winning the 1958 World Series, Stengal simply replied, "I couldn't have done it without my players."

Whether its Medicare, child care, health care, long-term care—or any other issue—we need each of you, and your organizations, to step up to the plate and help ensure that women's special needs are never overlooked. We need you to hold our feet to the fire. We need you to give us input and ideas. We need you to continue to stand up and speak out. And we need you to help remind everyone that women's issues are really family issues—and they're really national issues. It's thanks to organizations like yours that women's issues, women's interests, and women's rights have come so far. So I'm sure that, working together, we can help address the needs of every woman, every day, everywhere.

The NIH Mission and Minority Health[5]

Ruth Kirschstein, M.D.

Acting Director, National Institutes of Health (NIH), 2000– ; native of Brooklyn, N.Y.; B.A., Long Island University, 1947; M.D., Tulane University School of Medicine, 1951; research in experimental pathology, Division of Biologics Standards (now Center for Biologics Evaluation and Research, FDA), 1957–72; participant in World Health Organization deliberations, Geneva, Switzerland, 1965; consultant on problems related to the use of live poliovirus oral vaccine, 1967; assistant director and director, Division of Biologics Standards, 1972; director of the National Institute of General Medical Sciences (NIGMS), 1974–93; acting associate director, NIH for research on women's health, 1990–91; has received several health-related public service awards and honorary medical degrees.

Editors' introduction: Director Ruth Kirschstein addressed an audience of 800, including scientists, health care providers, and members of the Advisory Committee for Research on Minority Health, attending a conference on "Challenges in Health Disparities in the New Millennium: A Call to Action" sponsored by the National Institutes of Health Office of Research on Minority Health. She expressed concern about "health disparities between minority and majority populations, and what we intend to do in the future."

Ruth Kirschstein's speech: Good morning, everyone. I am delighted to join you, and honored to have been asked to open this conference.

This is a landmark event for the National Institutes of Health—and I applaud Dr. John Ruffin and his staff in the NIH Office of Research on Minority Health for the marvelous job they have done to make all this possible.

This conference marks not only the tenth anniversary of the office but also an important threshold in efforts by the NIH—and our partners—to expand research opportunities for minority scientists and to reduce or indeed eliminate disparities in health status among racial and ethnic minority groups by appropriate research endeavors.

---

5. Delivered in the Hyatt Regency Washington on Capitol Hill, Washington, D.C., at 8:45 a.m., on April 17, 2000. Reprinted with permission of Ruth L. Kirschstein.

Overcoming such persistent and perplexing health disparities, and promoting health for all Americans, particularly those who have suffered most, ranks as one of our foremost scientific challenges.

We have entered the 21st Century with such scientific and technological munificence that we *should* and *must*—and I stress *both words*—be able to promise good health and long life to all our citizens.

But, while for millions of Americans that promise is reality, for far too many it is not. Examples abound of what can be achieved:

You may have seen a story in the *Washington Post* last week reporting on a surgical team's work to correct spina bifida on an infant still in the womb.

At the other end of the age spectrum, more Americans than ever before in our history are living to celebrate their 100th birthday.

But you and I are here this morning because we know there are sadder stories to tell:

- We know that the number of African-American men and, particularly, women with AIDS has increased substantially.

- We know that Hispanic women are the least likely to use preventive services such as the Pap test, mammography, and clinical breast exam.

- We know that the prevalence rate of diabetes among American Indians and Alaska Natives is more than twice that for the total population. The Pima Indians of Arizona have the highest known prevalence of diabetes of any population in the world. And diabetes is also more prevalent in Hispanics and African Americans.

We can all add many more such stories from our own experiences. We are all well aware that disparities in health status among various populations in the United States are not only great, but appear to be growing—both with regard to premature death and to poorer general well-being.

It must be of deep concern to all of us that in some instances these disparities among population groups are widening—even as this Nation boasts of unprecedented progress in medical science.

All of us who have been privileged to participate in this age of robust scientific discovery have a responsibility to ensure that the new knowledge generated in our laboratories and our clinics benefits *all* our citizens and *all* our communities.

NIH Categories of Progress

So this morning, I want to talk to you about how the NIH is already addressing health disparities between minority and majority populations, and what we intend to do in the future.

The NIH is a complex enterprise, and our progress in identifying and addressing health disparities falls into several categories.

(1) The first is research into those diseases and disorders that disproportionately afflict minorities. This includes a number of cancers, diabetes, sickle cell disease, cardiovascular disease and hypertension, infant mortality, and autoimmune diseases such as lupus.

Of significance is the fact that active recruitment efforts have resulted in more minorities than ever before participating in NIH–supported clinical trials. We expect this number to grow as information about these studies becomes accessible to many more people through *clinicaltrials.gov*—our new on-line clinical trials database.

In addition, many of our Institutes and Centers have fostered research partnerships between institutions, in order to include more minorities in research and to bring the benefits of medical research and medical care to the patients in those institutions.

(2) The second category is professional and scientific training, with the goals of building research capacity, advancing the expertise of faculty, and attracting more underrepresented minority students to the sciences and to careers in medicine and research.

Success in this area has been painfully slow, a fact that we sadly acknowledge. However, we are beginning to see a glimmer of hope, because for the first time we may have the authority as well as some funds for a debt forgiveness program for students and trainees who will work in the area of health disparities.

We are also focusing on expanding the size and diversity of our own NIH work force and scientific staff.

(3) The third category of NIH endeavor is outreach, aimed at bringing information about treatment, prevention, and self-management of disease to the public through national health education campaigns and neighborhood or community programs.

Our aim at NIH is to promote the development and transfer of research-based information in the biomedical, behavioral, and social sciences for use by health professionals, communities, and others in working toward the elimination of health disparities.

DHHS Goals

We are building upon NIH's participation in the Department of Health and Human Services' program to reach the following six goals:

1. Improve infant health for racial and ethnic minorities, and eliminate disparities in the infant mortality rate—with special attention to Sudden Infant Death Syndrome

2. Eliminate disparities in breast, cervical, and prostate cancer screening and improve management of these cancers.

3. Eliminate disparities in and reduce cardiovascular disease, including hypertension rates.

4. Eliminate disparities in diabetes and reduce diabetes-related complications.

5. Eliminate disparities in and improve access to state of the art HIV testing, counseling, health care, and support services.

6. Childhood and adult immunizations.

Identifying Gaps

But this is not enough. We must identify other areas in which the gaps are as great or are widening—gaps which, through research, can be narrowed or eliminated. In some cases our approach, to be effective, requires basic and clinical research. In others, community outreach is needed. All our efforts will be directed toward reaching people most in need.

We know what happens when we put our best effort forward.

Last year, for example, NIH provided $1.2 million in support for minority health research. Let me give you some examples:

- The Jackson Heart Study, a prospective study of the environmental and genetic factors affecting the disproportionate incidence of cardiovascular diseases in African American men and women.

- Research into the impact of diabetes on minority populations, with special focus on clinical trials on prevention as well as studies of genetic and molecular mechanisms, pathogenesis, and new therapies.

- The Prostate, Lung, Colorectal, and Ovarian Cancer Screening Trial—a large randomized study designed to learn if certain screening tests will reduce the number of deaths from the cancers that significantly affect minorities.

- The Cooperative Study of Sickle Cell Disease—as well as other research on this illness—designed to further our understanding of the cellular and molecular mechanisms that might contribute to effective therapy.

- The Women's Health Initiative. This is a 14-year, $600+ million program that seeks definitive answers to key questions about cancer, heart disease, and osteoporosis.

NIH Working Group on Health Disparities

To strengthen and expand on these efforts, last September NIH established a working group on health disparities. The group was charged with assessing NIH's progress in reducing and eliminating health disparities, and determining the most effective methods of using NIH resources.

In December, the group made four preliminary recommendations:

1. Expand research on health disparities, as well as research training and employment opportunities for individuals likely to have a major interest in such research.

2. Define the scope and focus of the NIH health disparities program, and establish standard definitions so that monitoring, reporting, and analysis of data will have consistency and reliability.

3. Strengthen existing partnerships and create new links within and outside NIH—with other Department agencies and other sectors of society concerned with health disparities research.

4. Increase communication and transfer of knowledge from NIH to the many constituencies interested in improving the health of all Americans.

When I became Acting Director in January, I reconstituted this Trans–NIH Working Group. I appointed, as its members, all the Institute and Center Directors and I have held them accountable to attend all the meetings. As co-chairs, I appointed two senior NIH leaders: Dr. Anthony Fauci, Director of the National Institute of Allergy and Infectious Diseases; and Dr. Yvonne Maddox, my new Acting Deputy Director of NIH, and previously Deputy Director of the National Institute on Child Health and Human Development.

The group was charged to prepare—and now is preparing—an integrated strategic plan on health disparities for all of NIH. In addition, each Institute and Center, with its Advisory Council and constituency groups, is charged to prepare its own plan for addressing health disparities. However, the NIH plan will be much more than a simple compilation of the individual plans.

This Trans–NIH Strategic Plan for Research on Health Disparities will be developed through an open process with substantial public input, particularly from representatives of groups who disproportionately experience disparities in health. The plan will be sent to the Director of the NIH Office of Research on Minority Health who, along with his Advisory Committee, will review this Strategic Plan before it is sent to me for final approval.

The plan will provide NIH with programs to be incorporated into the FY 2002 budget request for NIH.

Each Institute and Center Director has personally pledged his or her support for this endeavor. And at my request, each addressed the issue of health disparities during recent appropriations hearings.

Call to Action

I know you all are aware of and assured of my personal commitment to this endeavor.

Today's conference provides a timely opportunity for me to publicly re-affirm *NIH's* commitment to bringing the full strength of its research and training programs to bear on the tasks of eliminating domestic health disparities, increasing participation by minorities in clinical research, and increasing substantially the number of minority clinical and basic medical scientists, who are essential to making our efforts a success.

As President Clinton emphasized in his State of the Union address and other recent speeches, it is in the national interest that major efforts be made to reduce health disparities.

So I challenge all of us, you and me here today, to join all at NIH—as colleagues and partners—in a determined effort to eliminate racial and ethnic health disparities and to expand research efforts and opportunities for scientists who are minorities.

I congratulate Dr. John Ruffin for his ten years of success as Director of the NIH Office of Research on Minority Health. I pledge my unwavering commitment to the programs to eliminate health disparities through research and to provide research opportunities to scientists who are minority, and to assuring that such programs have all the tools and authorities required to achieve even greater success in meeting the challenge.

This conference will set the goals for the "Call to Action in the New Millennium."

Thank you very much.

V. Technology and Ethics

The Challenge to Generation D:
Beyond the Color Line[1]

William E. Kennard

Chairman, Federal Communications Commission (FCC), 1997– ; born in Los Angeles, CA, January 19, 1957; B.A. (Phi Beta Kappa), Stanford University, 1978; J.D., Yale Law School, 1981; FCC's Advisory Committee on Minority Ownership in Broadcasting, 1980s; fellow, National Association of Broadcasters, Washington, 1981–82, assistant general counsel, 1983–94; law firm of Verner, Liipfert, Bernhard, McPherson, and Hand, Chartered, 1984–89, partner 1990–93; general counsel of the FCC, 1993–97; first African American to chair the FCC.

Editors' Introduction: In his commencement address to the Class of 2000 at Howard University, FCC Chairman Kennard urges the graduates to work towards closing the "gap between the information haves and haves-not . . . called the digital divide." As well-educated African Americans, he tells them, they are "required" to build a more inclusive society through service to their community.

William E. Kennard's speech: Thank you, President Swygert, and thank you, Chairman Savage, for this honor. I feel very privileged to address your commencement ceremony on this glorious day.

My congratulations to the graduates. I commend each of you—especially students graduating magna cum laude or summa cum laude or cum laude, and all the parents who are just thinking, "It's finally graduation day, thank you, Lordy"—I congratulate you all.

I did not attend Howard. But I am an heir to this institution. We all are. Because, each of us stands on the shoulders of those who walked the grounds of this special place.

We stand on the shoulders of Howard University President Mordecai Wyatt Johnson, who helped introduce Dr. Martin Luther King Jr. to nonviolence; and America became an heir to a revolution for social justice.

We stand on the shoulders of Howard University's Dr. Carter G. Woodson, who authored new chapters in the history of our people; and all Americans became heirs to a history as rich, as diverse, as compelling as those represented in this millennial graduating class.

---

1. Delivered on May 13, 2000, at Howard University, Washington, D.C.

We stand on the shoulders of Howard alumni Toni Morrison and Zora Neal Hurston. They painted a portrait of the African-American family; and all Americans became heirs to stories so rich, so textured, so lovingly detailed that they changed the face of 20th-century American literature.

We stand on the shoulders of Howard's Charles Hamilton Houston. He made the law school a civil rights citadel where lawyers like Thurgood Marshall, Vernon Jordan and President James Madison Nabrit Jr. were trained to battle for justice; and all Americans, all Americans, became heirs to laws that can, in the words of the prophet Amos, allow "justice to roll down like waters and righteousness like a mighty stream."

And we stand on the shoulders of Howard's Dr. Benjamin Hooks. He was a pioneer of civil rights as the head of the NAACP and the first African-American member of the Federal Communications Commission.

As the FCC's first African-American chairman, I stand on his shoulders.

I know one thing, I would not be standing before you today as Chairman of the FCC were it not for this institution.

Howard's story is our story, the story of African-American families.

We must recognize those most responsible for this graduation: the mothers and fathers, the grandmothers and grandfathers, the aunts and uncles.

These are the people who cosigned the student loans, loaded the U-Haul trucks, paid the tuition or promised to, those who sent the care packages and paid for the collect calls, who wired the money—who borrowed money from your aunt—who borrowed from your uncle—who gave the money to your mother—who pretended to loan it to you.

Today we recognize them all. As you graduate into this *.com economy, never, EVER forget those who taught you your ABC's.

Thinking about families, I cannot help but think about my own grandfather and the lessons he taught his family.

My grandfather—his name was James Kennard—worked on the network that formed the foundation of the Industrial Age. He was a Pullman porter on the railroads—it was in fact the best job a black man could have on the railroad in those days.

My grandfather was a brilliant man. A learned man. A beautiful writer. He could quote everything from the Bible to Shakespeare. And my grandfather was completely self-taught—a man whose only professor was his own curiosity.

And yet he rode the rails for years and could go nowhere. He could be a part of the most important industrial network of his time, so long as he stayed in his place as the man who carried the bags.

My grandfather wanted to find a better life for his family. So he left the segregated south and moved them to California.

But even in California, the black children would go to one school, the white children to another. It turns out that the black school was across town. The white school was a few blocks away.

When my father was five, my grandfather sent him off to the neighborhood school. And they sent my dad home.

The principal said, "Colored children can't go to this school."

The next day, my grandfather dressed my father up and sent him back to that school. And they sent him home again. My grandfather said, "You belong there." So he sent him back again. And again. It was tough on my dad—kids used to chase him home and throw rocks at him. But he was quick and wiry—like me. So he made it.

And finally, the principal relented. "Okay," he said. "We'll take the Kennard boy."

My grandfather taught my dad that when the doors of opportunity are closed, you knock. And when nobody answers, you keep knocking. And if nobody answers that door of opportunity, then you break that door down and walk on through.

My grandfather taught his son to smash through glass ceilings maintained by the insecure and the incompetent. My grandfather taught his son that when a road block lies in your path, you drive under it, around it, through it, over it—that you let nothing stand in the way of your dreams.

That was my grandfather's lesson to my father and my father's lesson to me. And I know it is Howard's lesson to you.

Today you receive degrees in your diverse fields—engineering, literature, medicine, and law. But you go forth from this campus as more than specialists in any field. You are heirs to a tradition—a tradition that teaches us we can do anything we dream and demands that we bring everyone along.

It's a powerful tradition embodied in your motto: "Leadership for America and the Global Community."

Now this tradition certainly echoes in the story of Andrew Young.

Andy is another distinguished graduate of this institution—an heir to this tradition. Andy is a pioneer of the civil rights movement. He was a mayor—a congressman—an ambassador to the United Nations.

For Andy Young, a lifetime of achievement began by asking one question. In his memoir, *An Easy Burden*, he tells the story that after three years at Howard of not seriously applying himself, he had the uneasy feeling that he was not doing all that he could with what he had.

In the summer before his senior year at Howard, Andy returned to his hometown of New Orleans. He ran into an old friend named Lincoln. They talked about the different paths they had taken in life.

Despite growing up at the same time, in the same community, they didn't have the same opportunity.

Andy's mother and father were able to send him to college. Lincoln's mother struggled to raise eight children by herself. While Andy was looking forward to a life of new opportunity, Lincoln had dropped out of school. One thing led to another, and he finally ended up in jail.

> *The promise of this digital era is not just building smarter devices. It is building stronger communities.*

Andy returned to Howard unable to put Lincoln out of his mind. Thinking about Lincoln, a verse from the book of Luke tugged at Andy's soul:

"To whom much is given, much is required."

And Andy asked himself: "What will be required of me?"

We all know that Andy Young answered that question with words and work, declaration and deeds, a lifetime of service and sacrifice.

And that brings me to my challenge for this graduating class—for you the heirs to the tradition of Howard—this tradition of producing leaders for America and the global community.

To whom much is given, much is required.

Much has been given to you. I call you GENERATION D, the digital generation. You will graduate into a world where the Internet will give you instantaneous access to global markets; where you can use a device that you will hold in the palm of your hand to access more information than is contained in the Howard University library. And I know you will go forward to invent even greater technologies and with them you will achieve what we cannot even imagine today.

But the promise of this digital era is not just building smarter devices. It is building stronger communities.

Technology cannot give every American access to opportunity until every American has access to technology.

At the dawn of the last century, W. E. B. DuBois said, "the problem of the 20th century is the problem of the color line." At the dawn of this century, our challenge is to make sure that the color line does not determine who is on-line.

Thirty-five years ago, President Lyndon Johnson stood here and delivered a landmark address on civil rights.

He said those now famous words: "You cannot take a person who, for years, has been hobbled by chains and liberate him, bring him up to the starting line of a race and then say, 'You are free to compete with all the others,' and still justly believe that you have been completely fair."

What Lyndon Johnson said 35 years ago is even more true today. Because today the race is being run on Internet time. The race track is a global network of fiber-optic lines, broadband cables and wireless connections over which ones and zeroes race at Internet speed. Those who start behind will stay behind—and this race runs so fast they will never catch up.

And we are already off to an uneven start. Blacks and Hispanics are only 40 percent as likely as whites to have Internet access at home. This gap between the information haves and haves-not is called the digital divide.

Now some people argue there is no digital divide. In fact, it is an argument brought to you by the same folks who say we live in a color-blind society. Frankly, I don't know what country those people live in. It certainly isn't the America I know.

That is why I have devoted my tenure at the FCC to bridging this divide of opportunity—to preventing the color line from deciding who is on-line—to ensuring that every American has access to the tools of the 21st century.

I believe that ensuring that all Americans have access to technology is the civil rights challenge of this new millennium.

We will not meet this challenge until all of our children are as interested in becoming Michael Dell as they are in becoming Michael Jordan—when they would rather have the latest laptops than the latest high-tops.

And for me, meeting that challenge—embracing public service—has been the most exhilarating experience of my life.

I have seen the faces of children in our inner cities light up as they surf the Web for the first time and then I've known the reward of crafting the policies that will wire a million classrooms to the Internet.

Thanks to the vision of President Clinton and Vice President Gore, since 1997 this country has invested 10 billion dollars to connect our schools to the Internet. It's a program called the E-rate.

And I am proud to say that in three years we have wired one million classrooms to the Internet, improving the lives of 40 million American children.

And I have visited the homes of Native Americans on reservations in New Mexico and Arizona. Too many of them are still waiting for a telephone. I heard their stories too. They told me about what it is like to live in the 21st century without a telephone, when you can't call your doctor or an ambulance or the police.

Then I've known the satisfaction of working with my FCC colleagues on proposals to bring basic telephone service to over a million low-income Indian people on tribal lands.

What is required of you? Not merely net worth but the wealth of character that declares across this yawning digital divide: leave no one behind, bring everyone along.

I have had the privilege of meeting almost every one of the CEOs of the high-tech sector—these 20- and 30-something billionaires who, overnight, have created almost unimaginable wealth. And, you know, not one of those CEOs who have walked through my door is African-American, and that has got to change. And you are going to change it.

I have heard the stories of Americans with disabilities who worry that this Internet revolution will pass them by and then celebrated with them as we created the rules to ensure that they will have access to this wondrous technology.

I am proud of the work that we have done to bring all Americans into the Information Age together—to bridge the digital divide. But we have only just begun. And what my generation has done is but a prelude to what this generation can do—as heirs to the Howard tradition. So I want to leave you with one question: what is required of you?

What is required of you? The very same determination that enabled your families here today to put sacrifice before self, to put your tuition before their vacations, your graduation before their retirement.

What is required of you? Not merely net worth but the wealth of character that declares across this yawning digital divide: leave no one behind, bring everyone along.

What is required of you? Not merely a degree but the knowledge that a Howard University diploma means that you are not only qualified to compete but blessed to serve.

What is required of you? Service. So much so, the legacy of the Howard tradition bears eloquent witness to the truth of the poet who wrote:

No vision and you perish;
No ideal, and you're lost;
Your heart must ever cherish,
Some faith at any cost.
Some hope, some dream to cling to,
Some rainbow in the sky,
Some melody to sing to,
Some service that is high.

What is required of you? That when the call is heard, to answer in the words of the prophet Isaiah, "Here I am. Send me."

What is required of you? To heed the book of Ephesians, "Having done all to stand, just stand."

And now having studied, worked, saved, persevered, persisted through sacrifice and dreamed simply stand.

As you receive your diplomas today, stand.

Stand with my grandfather.

Stand with your mothers.

Stand with your fathers.

Stand with all the members of your family.

Stand with your classmates.

Stand with your professors.

And stand with the untold multitude of Howard alumni who brought you to where you are—that you might lead this nation to where it should be.

Congratulations and thank you very much.

Stop the Suffering—End Online Child Pornography[1]

Kathryn Walt Hall

U.S. Ambassador to Austria, 1997– ; raised in Texas; A.B. in economics, University of California, Berkeley; J.D., University of California Hastings College of Law; president, Kathryn Hall Vineyards, Inc., and Walt Management, Inc., an inner-city housing and development company; managing director and partner, Hall Financial Group, Inc.; assistant city attorney, Berkeley, CA; with Safeway Stores, developed affirmative action program; attorney and businesswoman, Dallas, TX; served on boards addressing social care and mental health; U.S. House of Representatives Hunger Advisory Committee; director and vice president, Texas Mental Health Association; National Advisory Council for Violence Against Women, 1995; trustee of Woodrow Wilson International Center for Scholars.

Editors' introduction: In this speech to the Salzburg Women's Career Network and the Austro-American Society, Ambassador Kathryn Walt Hall addressed approximately 150 professional women from government, academia, business, and media on the benefits and dangers of the Internet. While "users can access an almost limitless array of rewarding content" on the Internet, Ambassador Hall reminded them, at the same time, "children continue to be exposed to the risks and abuses currently occurring online." In the speech, Ambassador Hall also referred to the Conference "Combating Child Pornography on the Internet" that took place in Vienna, September 29–October 1, 1999.

Kathryn Walt Hall's speech:

Introduction (The good news)

As we dash toward the second millennium, the Internet has forever changed the way we play, buy, educate, communicate and dream. But, in the tumultuous and extraordinary year of 1969, the quiet birth of the Internet—which allowed computers to talk to one another—had some pretty tough competition for media coverage.

It was a year that ended the decade of the 60s with a bang . . . and the world has never been quite the same:

---

1. Delivered in Salzburg, Austria, on September 21, 1999, addressing the Salzburg Women's Career Network and the Austro-American Society. Reprinted with permission of Kathryn Walt Hall.

It was a year that ended the decade of the 60s with a bang . . . and the world has never been quite the same:

- A rock concert on a farm in upstate New York makes "Woodstock" the most famous small town in the world, spurring numerous "reunions" but never one that worked as well as the original.

- While Jimmy Hendrix played the Star Spangled Banner on electric guitar with his teeth, the U.S. prime interest rate was soaring three times, hitting 8.5%.

- It was safer to fly the Friendly Skies in 1999 then it was in 1969, when airplane hijackings around the world occurred 65 times.

- Neil Armstrong becomes the first man to walk on the moon.

- Breaking the heart of every teenage girl around the world, the "cute" Beatle Paul McCartney marries Linda Eastman while John Lennon and Yoko Ono tie the knot and get political.

- IBM unbundles its software products for the first time, allowing customers to buy software separately from its computers. Thereby, creating the software market—setting the stage for the growth of Silicon Valley and for a Harvard dropout by the name of Bill Gates to become the wealthiest man in the U.S., three decades later.

Internet Benefits & Revolutionary Positive Changes

This month, celebrating its 30th birthday, the Internet remains a youngster by technological standards. And yet, it has been called the most profound change in the way we communicate since the invention of the printing press.

Users can access an almost limitless array of rewarding content at the click of a mouse, and they are doing so in vast and surprising numbers:

- There are over 350 million personal computers today with Internet capability. Most people today buy computers simply so they can log on to the Net.

- Over 100 million global user's "login" into the Internet daily, and this is expected to increase to 515 million by 2002.

- Sales over the Internet could top one trillion dollars in just a few years.

- E-mail addresses are as common as street addresses for 54% of the American households now hooked up to the Web.

- 39% of all Americans are on-line, that's about 76 million compared to Europe's 16%. 31% of all Austrians, or 2 million Austrian's, now have Internet accessibility. Austria is number 3 in Europe behind Sweden with 49% usage and Norway with 48%.

- The real growth in the use of the Internet is outside of the United States. 45% of Internet users live in Europe and Southeast Asia and this number will double in two years.

As the Internet becomes a familiar technology to millions of users, a whole new set of words have entered our daily vocabulary; login, Information Highway, the Global Village, Worldwide Web, the Net, ISPs or Internet Service Providers, Gateways, Websites, Homepages, download, e-mail, chatrooms, search engines, pop-ups, encryption devices, Amazon.com, Yahoo.com and Cyberspace.

And it's not just the new vocabulary but the new opportunities and unparalleled convenience that makes the Internet truly the medium of communication for the future:

- If you are from Dallas, Texas, but live in Salzburg, Austria, you can download your hometown newspaper, the *Dallas Morning News*, keeping abreast of people and events that matter to you, effectively closing the "distance gap."

- Or on the other hand if you live in Dallas and miss Salzburg, you can order Austrian food specialties through the Internet as you may have read in the *Salzburger Nachricten*—the specialties should soon be available on-line.

- If you want to get an advanced degree, and your German isn't quite ready for university-level work, you now have the option of taking classes on-line from the University of New York or from my alma mater, the University of California at Berkeley.

- Keeping in touch with children, friends or parents abroad is a snap with e-mail—in most cases a lot more convenient and cheaper than a phone call.

- Want information about America? Want to read speeches by American officials, get travel warnings, or just learn more about the American Embassy in Austria? Visit our Web-site at www.usembassy-vienna.at or chat with us the first or third Wednesday of each month.

- If you're flying to London, you can check the weather or read the reviews of the musical that opened yesterday in the west end.

- No time for grocery shopping . . . my most dreaded job while I was living in the states? Order it over the Internet from your local grocery store and have it delivered. Meinl grocery store in Austria is on-line and they do deliver!

- It's 9 o'clock at night, the library is closed, and your teenager has just started her research paper due tomorrow morning. She has a good chance she can finish it—if she hops onto any of the search engines on the Net—AND doesn't spend the first two hours sending e-mails to her girlfriends!

Introduction to Internet & Kids & Dark Side

Familiarity with this technology is vital to our children's future. The Internet can entertain and empower our children. For today's children to lead tomorrow's world, they must acquire the skills to access the enormous benefits of the Internet. It is especially important that they develop the key job skills and an awareness of the increasingly global community. The Internet can give them the ability to communicate, and to share ideas and information on a worldwide basis.

All of this creative and innovative growth offers tremendous convenience and unrealized potential for the on-line community—of

---

The Internet's dark side has spawned yet another set of additions to our lexicon: Cybercrime, cyberchild porn, hotlines, cybercriminals and cybercops.

---

which our children and their children—will become the major beneficiaries. Still, with every new technological gift capable of altering our world and lives with its light and brilliance, there is contained a shadow flip side to this coin of fortune.

One of the fathers of the Internet, Professor Richard Kleinrock from UCLA says, "Thirty years ago, I never imagined 'the dark side of the Internet'—with all that porn and all that hate." Unfortunately, the Internet's dark side has spawned yet another set of additions to our lexicon: Cybercrime, cyberchild porn, hotlines, cybercriminals and cybercops.

Along with the bright future for this Internet youngster, we must sadly acknowledge that there is an Enfant Terrible lurking inside every computer with an Internet connection, as pedophiles and pornographers peddle their illegal trade in cyberspace, causing untold damage to those most vulnerable in society—our children. Additional problems include equitable access, marketing and advertising practices, quality content and privacy along with implementing effective policies and policing against cybercriminals who stalk and abuse our children over the Net.

Internet Crimes & Abuses against Children

Today, there are 17 million children worldwide surfing the Internet. As the Internet grows, so do the risks to our children by being exposed to inappropriate material, and in particular, to criminal activity by pedophiles and child pornographers. No country, no family, and no child is safe from these dangers in the borderless world of cyberspace:

Several weeks ago in Austria, five people were arrested for trafficking in illegal child pornography over the Internet.

In Germany, a Berlin doctor was sentenced to two years in prison for distributing over 9,000 pornographic photos over the Internet of children; some with animals and depicting scenes of violence.

In England, a Catholic priest was sentenced to six years in prison after he was found guilty of sexually abusing young boys and exchanging pornographic materials with a pedophile ring on the Internet.

In the Netherlands, police busted a child pornography ring that tied children up; raped and abused them on camera then distributed the video over the Internet so that others could watch. One of these children was a 12-year-old boy who had disappeared in Berlin five years ago and is still missing.

In San Jose, California, Ronald Riva admitted to sexually molesting a 10-year-old girl, filming the incident with his digital camera then immediately posting the pictures on an International online child pornography ring called The Orchid Club. Riva was one of sixteen Orchid Club members sentenced to jail. He is currently serving a thirty-year prison sentence.

Riva is now safely behind bars but he and the others I have just mentioned are the few who are caught—the rest hide in cyberspace.

The sickening truth is that the vast majority of cyberchild pornography crimes remain unreported and unchecked in spite of a 410% increase in the prosecution of child pornography over the Internet. The FBI reports over 4,000 cases of child pornography being distributed on-line in the United States. 23,000 web sites have already been detected as advocating sex with children.

Risks of Internet for Children

As a result, thousands of children worldwide are believed to have suffered sexual abuse by members of cyberpedophilia rings that stretch from the U.S. to the European Union and beyond. For these young victims, the real dangers include: contracting sexually transmitted diseases, rape, assault, torture, and even, and if they survive the physical harm their emotional wounds nevertheless remain. If left untreated, often those abused create another generation of child abusers.

Children are sexually exploited repeatedly every time their images are transmitted on the Internet. Once their photograph appears on the Internet, it is almost impossible to remove it. In the U.S. alone, there are over 500,000 online photos showing sexual acts involving minors.

The nature of the Internet makes it easy for children to access obscene materials and become prey to cybercriminals.

This visual documentation of the child's exploitation causes a deep sense of shame and guilt in the child and fear that their family or friends might discover the exploitation. This fear often makes it difficult for a child who has been exploited to testify in court against the molester.

Children continue to be exposed to the risks and abuses currently occurring on-line because the nature of the Internet makes it easy for children to access obscene materials and become prey to cybercriminals. Children do so in a number of ways:

- Often, they mistakenly mistyped URLs (Uniform Resource Locators).

- Using common search engines to look for innocent information often brings in links to pornographic sites as well. For example searches for "toys," "pets," "boys," "girls," and even "Barney" all bring links to porn sites among others. The need to constantly say "NO" battles with a child's natural curiosity.

- Misdirected searches

- "Push" pornography and e-mailed links—with recent developments in technology, content can be "pushed" to intended recipients either through special interactive applications or as links contained in e-mails. Children open their e-mail and find direct access to adult content sites. Many e-mails bear subject lines that can be very deceptive, and children can't determine their contents merely by looking at the subject line.

- If a child, out of curiosity or carelessness, clicks on such links, the result will often be either a pornographic image or heavy four-lettered language. Once children are exposed to this material, it can never be erased from their minds.

- In the anonymous chat room, cybercriminals most often search for their next young victims.

Internet Perpetrators

And while the Internet has not caused the problem, it has provided a safe haven for pornographers and pedophiles to sexually abuse our children by contacting them and distributing child pornography through the anonymity of the Internet. One out of every four adults in North American has access to the Internet. In 2000, 90% of all American students in school will have access to the Net creating a much larger pool of potential victims for pedophiles and child pornographers to draw from.

The Internet facilitates the duplication and recycling of old materials, shortening the time between production and distribution through the use of cheaper and easily accessible new technologies like digital cameras, scanners and photo file software. These technologically savvy cybercriminals elude authorities by concealing themselves through a maze of Internet servers, providers, files, screen names and sophisticated encryption devices. They always seem to be one step ahead of the law.

Who are Cyberchild pornographers? According to the FBI, 99% are white, professional males, 25-45 years of age. They are above average in intelligence, own a computer and most have no prior arrests for pedophilia. Child pornography is produced, collected and used by pedophiles mainly their own sexual arousal and gratification. New studies show that the proliferation of child pornography over the Internet has given new life to this old vice.

One of the most important things in a pedophile's life is his collection of pornography. FBI Special Agent, Pete Gulotti says, "These guys collect child pornography like stamp collectors collect stamps. They all want the fresh, new ones, and to find new stuff. They're always looking for something that nobody else has, always raising the stakes. There are tens of thousands of these photographs going around the Internet every day. In my 30 years with the FBI, I've worked over 300 violations, and child pornographers are the most reprehensible group I've ever had to investigate."

Their operations are underground and restricted. They mostly deal with known pedophile customers. To become a member in a child pornography online club, the new member is usually required to send one or more original pornographic photos on-line. Once the child pornography is acquired, the pedophile carefully organizes and adds to his collection by storing the image on back-up tapes and computer disks, often using advanced computer technology to hide the illegal file.

Pedophiles don't just use the pornography for themselves; they use the child pornography they have collected to seduce other children into participating with them in sexual activities by lowering the inhibitions of potential victims. When shown images of other children performing sexual acts, these children are led to believe that participation in sexually explicit behavior is acceptable, making it easier for the pedophile to molest the child.

How does a pornographer or pedophile contact a child on the Internet? Police and the press report that pedophiles are using chat rooms to lure children into physical meetings. According to a recent newspaper report, chat rooms are the most popular activity for children on-line, yet most chat rooms are unsupervised. Many are "private" accessible only by invitation and special passwords which may be provided to children by e-mail or "instant-type" messages to the screen of a targeted child.

Through chat rooms, adult strangers can have direct access to our children. The "safe" home setting, combined with our children's natural trust, may lead them to forget that these people are strangers. This makes it easier for the pedophile to prey on children who would never talk to a stranger in the "real word." The anonymity of Internet chat rooms, and the code names and encryption devices used on the Net, make it very difficult for law enforcement agencies to catch these perpetrators and stop their insidious crimes.

Introduction to Policing the Internet & Parents

Only 382 cases have been successfully tried in the United States, the vast majority of these child pornographers are free to continue trafficking in child smut. However, authorities are closing ranks as parents, educators, industry officials along with the international community has started placing a higher priority on this growing problem.

Assuring that the Internet is safe for our children has become a major issue for every parent in all countries with Internet access. Yet, some Civil liberty groups, Internet users and even, many in the Internet industry have battled against "control" and "regulation" of the Internet. They argue—with some validity—those basic human rights such as freedom of expression, speech and privacy are essential in democratic countries and to the continued growth of the Internet. But criminal activity on-line should not and cannot be tolerated.

All of our children are precious. Their safety on-line is our responsibility. It is time to stop their suffering from this revolting crime. Cyberstalkers invade your living room through your computer, and they can operate in your home without your permission.

The last line of defense rests with parental supervision and control, and by educating every child to the dangers and risks of the Internet.

The U.S. Custom's office and the FBI have published a brochure presenting several steps that assist parents in keeping their children safe on the Internet:

- Placing any computer with Internet access in a central area of the house, not in a child's bedroom or secluded area.

- Cautioning children not to give out personal information such as their full names, address or telephone numbers to anyone on the Net without parental permission.

- Not permitting face-to-face meetings with people met on the Net, unless they are in a public place and a parent is present.

- Getting to know your children's on-line friends.

- Not allowing on-line profiles or personal web pages that give out your children's personal information, such as age, school, town, etc.

- Reporting any child pornography to the hotlines, which are connected to the proper legal authorities within the countries they operate.

- Becoming knowledgeable about the tools in the digital toolbox— or user employment tools includes codes of conduct to guide the development of the Internet.

A list of software tools and parental control options includes software such as CyberPatrol, Net Nanny, Surf Watch, Cybersitter and Softeyes, among others, which block "bad sites" from appearing on your home computer as well as "keyword" preferences set by parents. Although these software "filter" features are only a partial solution, they are no substitute for parental oversight . . . or for increased cooperation by governments and law enforcement agencies. There are also hotlines available to report problems or ask for help. The hotline address in Austria is http://www.hotline.ispa.at.

International Cooperation Efforts

President Clinton has announced an expansive plan to build a family-friendly Internet by giving children a "seat belt" for cyberspace. The White House plan called for cooperation from the Internet industry to provide parents and teachers with "easy-to-use" child protection technology that includes new software designed to protect children in cyberspace.

This is not a problem of one nation. The United States is cooperating with other countries, realizing that our common responsibilities and the devastating social consequences of this child abuse. To successfully stop this abhorrent crime, we must work together—not just within our own households—but with our neighbors down the street and even, around the world.

- The U.S. Customs Service is working closely with the Austrian Ministry of Interior in identifying and prosecuting perpetrators of child pornography. Our Customs Service has also trained several Austrian law enforcement officials in investigating methods used to track down the crime of the 21st century.

- Internet Service Providers from many different countries are working together to establish voluntary self-regulation.

- The Internet Content Rating Association, composed of Internet Service Providers from many countries, was created in May of this year to develop a user friendly and culturally objective international Internet content rating system that protects children and fundamental freedoms on the web.

- International cooperation between hotline operators is growing, especially through the work of INHOPE (International Hotline Providers in Europe) Forum, a non-profit organization that promotes the work of national hotlines.

- Law enforcement authorities are discussing setting up an international network of national monitoring units used to filter out material, which shows victims and perpetrators who were already identified in the past.

- Interpol is advocating the harmonization of national laws dealing with child pornography to facilitate prosecution. Interpol also works on promoting international police cooperation.

To continue the international efforts I've just mentioned and put the problem into "hyper space mode," a joint U.S.–EU sponsored conference will be held in Vienna on September 29th through October 1st to combat child pornography over the Internet.

Initiated last year by U.S. Secretary of State Madeleine Albright and Austrian Foreign Minister Wolfgang Schuessel, the conference brings together policy makers, Internet Providers, hotline providers, enforcement and justice officials. Our goal is to facilitate an international framework for policing the Internet, encouraging the Internet providers to self-regulate while preserving fundamental liberties.

Over 300 participants from Western and Central Europe, the United States, Russia, Ukraine, Japan, China, Brazil, Canada, Australia, New Zealand and Argentina along with all major U.S. Internet providers, will gather at the Hofburg Palace in Vienna with a specific set of objectives and working groups to:

- Reinforce cooperation between cross-border law enforcement and the judiciary agencies

- Encourage Internet Service Providers to establish more rigorous self-regulatory mechanisms that cut-short the access of child pornographers and pedophiles to peddle their illegal trade

- Encourage the establishment of additional hotlines and networking to report crimes by citizens and pass this information along to law enforcement officials wherever the crime is committed.

But government and industry cannot do the job alone. As President Clinton says so often, "In the end, the responsibility for our children's safety will rest largely with their parents. With a combination of technology, law enforcement and parental responsibilities, we have the best chance to ensure that the Internet will be both safe for our children and the greatest educational resource we have ever known."

Thank you for your time and for the opportunity to share with you how the U.S. government in cooperation with the Austrian government is leading the way to stop child pornography on the Internet . . . assuring that our children have the right to a safe and enjoyable online experience.

The Dark Side of Technology[2]

Morality in the Information Age

Bill Joy

Co-founder and corporate executive officer, Sun Technologies, 1982– ; chief scientist, at Sun Microsystems, 1998– ; born 1954; B.S., electrical engineering, University of Michigan, 1975; M.S., electrical engineering and computer science, University of California–Berkeley, 1982; designed Sun's Network File System (NFS); co-designed SPARC microprocessor architecture; has driven the initial business and technical strategy for Java; recent work on human-computer interaction, new microprocessor and system architectures, and advances in complex adaptive systems, quantum computing, and the cognitive sciences; co-chair, Presidential Information Technology Advisory Committee (PITAC), 1997; member National Academy of Engineering; fellow, American Academy of Arts and Sciences; has received several awards for his work in computer design and engineering.

Editors' introduction: In a speech before 200 at the Commonwealth Club of California, Chief Scientist Bill Joy first explained how new "technologies will bring . . . almost unimaginable wealth." Then he cautioned that "we have a new situation . . . where the moral equivalent of the weapons of mass destruction may be available to people sitting at their personal computers." The address was carried over National Public Radio and C-SPAN.

Bill Joy's speech: Albert Einstein said that the unleashed power of the atom changed everything except our way of thinking, and that we were drifting toward unparalleled catastrophe. He was speaking of the threat of nuclear weapons approximately 40 years ago.

Today I want to talk to you about another threat that I see, but let me start by saying that I come here, fundamentally, because I'm an optimist about three new technologies: genetic engineering, nanotechnology and robotics (GNR). These technologies will bring us enormous benefits, creating almost unimaginable wealth. Genetic engineering will give us the ability to cure many diseases and extend our life spans. Nanotechnology promises to allow us to build material goods at much lower costs, certainly providing us the resources to end material poverty. And robotics may, within

---

2. Delivered on June 6, 2000, at 7:00 p.m. Reprinted with permission of Bill Joy.

this century, allow us to end most manual labor. There may well be tens of thousands of dot-geno, dot-robo and dot-nano startups that create this unimaginable wealth and provide a lot of opportunity for bright people.

These benefits come about because of the confluence of the physical and biological sciences with the field that I practice in: information technology. It's the ability to take information, say about genetics, and reduce it to a sequence of letters that can be manipulated in the computer to allow us to do some of these things. It's the continuation of a phenomenon in computing called Moore's Law that is a huge enabler. Moore's Law says that computing has been getting cheaper and will continue to get cheaper and more powerful.

Many people thought this trend would run out around 2010, but new technology that I learned about in detail last year, called nano or molecular electronics, now promises that we'll see this trend almost certainly continue to 2030. This would mean that by 2030 we should have inexpensive personal computers that are about a million times as powerful as they are today. These computers would allow people, with the information models in them, to begin to redesign the world in a very fundamental way.

A factor of a million is an almost inconceivable number. A calculation that would take 1,000 years on a computer today, on a computer of 2030 is likely to finish in something like eight hours, a calculation that would take a year would take 20 seconds. And we can also expect another factor of a million in improvement from algorithms, from the ways in which we solve very difficult problems. For total improvement in 30 years, perhaps on large-scale problems of 10^{12}, a million million, which is about the ratio of the power of an atomic weapon to a match head. Clearly, these advances have enormous implications and provide a lot of creative opportunity for bright people.

I believe that our culture is rooted in the Greeks. We've been running an experiment in freedom in civilization for 2500 years, with some interruptions like the Dark Ages. But our experiment restarted in a relatively happy way with the Renaissance, and science and technology have been creating wonderful things for the last 100 or 200 years and progress has been accelerating.

The Greeks were both spiritual and objective—Edith Hamilton, in her classic book *The Greek Way*, said, "The Greeks weren't tempered to evade facts. It's we ourselves who are the sentimentalists. We to whom poetry and art are only superficial decorations of life. The Greeks looked straight at life—they were completely unsentimental. It was a Roman who said it was sweet to die for one's country. The Greeks never said it was sweet to die for anything. They had no vital lies." I think, to be worthy of this tradition that we're the inheritors of, we have to be unsentimental when facing problems and dangers like we face. We have to be blunt if necessary, sometimes even unpleasant, and talk very honestly about our situation in the same way that they did that led to their great progress.

In the 20th century, we spent a lot of time dealing with nuclear, biological and chemical weapons. Clearly, if you follow the news, you see that these problems continue. These were technologies developed by the military; they had largely military uses with little commercial value, requiring large-scale activities and often rare raw materials to make the weapons and create new trouble using these technologies. In particular, the knowledge about how to do this was not widely available, at least, not for a long time. The truly dangerous stuff with the ability to destroy civilization was actually held by a couple of nation-states: the U.S. and the former Soviet Union.

The technologies of concern in the 21st century— GNR—are quite different. They're being developed by the commercial sector; they have both military and commercial uses and huge commercial value. As they

> *The moral equivalent of the weapons of mass destruction may be available to people sitting at their personal computers.*

become information sciences and are practicable on small computers, even personal computers, they no longer require the large-scale facilities that the earlier 20th century technologies did. If we're not careful, on the course we're on, the knowledge to do work in these fields will be widely—essentially universally—available.

The dangerous situation that we face is that as practice in these sciences becomes information and all information is available, then the weapon kind of information will be available, as well. That is, in an information age, if everything is information, weapons are information, also. We have a new situation that we haven't faced before, where the moral equivalent of the weapons of mass destruction may be available to people sitting at their personal computers, or even to small groups.

How can an individual do damage on such a large scale? Well, if you make a bomb, you can blow it up once. But if you make something that can replicate in the world and you release it, you can create harm far beyond the scale of the act that released it into the world. The technologies that can be created by GNR can self-replicate. So a single act, with these new kinds of knowledge-enabled massive destructive technologies, can cause extreme harm.

By combining the enormous computing power that is released by these new technologies—these million times faster computers—with the manipulative advances in the physical sciences, using these tools to manipulate what we understand about genetics and the physical world, we are releasing enormous transformative power. This power is certainly sufficient to redesign the world in a very fundamental way, for better or for worse, because the kind of replicating and evolving processes that have been confined to the natural world are now within the realms of human endeavor. The danger is that we know there are evil people in the world and, if we democratize access to all this knowledge so that everyone has these tools and they can then release self-replicating things, we have a recipe for disaster.

We're accustomed to living with almost routine scientific break-throughs, but we haven't come to terms with the fact that these technologies pose a different threat than the technologies that have come before. Uncontrolled self-replication of these new technologies can create enormous damage in the physical world. I don't think it's an exaggeration to say that we're on the course to the perfection of extreme evil, basically allowing evil to spread well beyond that which the weapons of mass destruction bequeath to the nation-states, to empowering this for extreme individuals.

To talk specifically about genetic engineering, the danger here is that the same technologies which can be used to cure many diseases and extend our life span, may allow people to go so far as to design their own disease, what one might call a "designer pathogen." If you ask the experts in this field, they're not exactly sure when this would be possible, but 20 years would be a good guess.

Diseases that are designed in the lab have no natural limits on their virulence. They needn't be weak because they're widespread; they can wipe out the species that is their target—there's no Dar-winian kind of principle that would prevent that even in the natural world. They certainly don't apply to things that we design in the lab. The virulence, contagion, and incubation period of such a disease could easily be engineered. What barrier would there be to someone given almost perfect knowledge of the world gotten from genetic engineering? If all the information is published, the equipment's getting cheaper, the computers are becoming almost infinitely pow-erful for design, and a good versus a bad design is simply a question of a sequence. This is a situation we have to avoid.

Nanotechnology is simply any technology practiced at the atomic scale. Instead of using only biological materials, nanotechnology uses any element in the periodic table and essentially mechanical kinds of designs and has a similar problem with an out of control replicator that the nanotech people call "gray goo." In response to the article that I wrote in *Wired,* one of the people involved in nanomedicine wrote an analysis of this—it's on the foresight.org Web site—and it's clear that it's not impossible that such replicators might, say, eat the biosphere, which is the particular analysis of this paper.

These kinds of things, in general, have been called pestilences in the world of our ancestors, but they are beyond our experience. I don't think that, in our living memory, we've seen things like this happen in the world. In the 14th century in Europe, we had the plague. The *Encyclopedia Britannica* says that it was transmitted to Europeans when a Kipchak army, besieging a Genoese trading post in the Crimea, catapulted plague-infested corpses into the town and, subsequently, a third of Europe's population died. Other people might say that the disease was actually transmitted by rats running off the ship, but that was clearly the intent—to use plague as a weapon. In the 16th century in the Americas, a similar thing happened with smallpox. Robert Wright, in his book *Stolen Continents,* said: "The turning point, as so often with the conquest of America, came with the Plague. The scourge was no longer left in the hands of God. Lord Jeffery Amherst secured his place in history as the inventor of modern germ warfare with this notorious command: 'Infect the Indians with sheets upon which smallpox patients have been lying, or by any other means which may serve to exterminate this accursed race.'" The last fast-moving pandemic that we had, I think, was the influenza epidemic of 1918, which is almost certainly out of our living collective memory.

This century, we've had advances in antibiotics and sanitation that have prevented most of these kinds of things from occurring, at least for a while. To try to bring back some memory of these things, I'd like to read you an abridged passage from the Roman Lucretius, the book *The Way Things Are,* the last chapter, describing a plague on Athens. He says:

> A plague once visited Athens. At first, they felt their heads burning with fever, throats blackened, sweating blood. The tongue filled up, engorged with blood, became too hard to move. Men's inner parts were burning to their very bones; their guts were furnaces. The only thing they had to drink was thirst, which made a deluge seem less than a raindrop. Doctors shook their heads while patients stared blankly. The signs of death were obvious; the mind was crazed with grief and fear. Eight days or nine would find the limbs grow stiff in death. There seemed to be no certain remedy; what gave life to one killed others. This plague was most infectious; it could spread as pestilences do with animals, cattle and sheep. So death was piled on death. None were left, sometimes, as mourners when the dead were hurried to their graves. Battles broke out as the survivors fought for funeral pyres of corpses heaped on corpses. Funeral rites, which these pious people held in all-traditional

reverence, became quite out of fashion. Everyone in grief buried his own whatever way he could amidst the general panic. Sudden need and poverty persuaded men to use horrible makeshifts. Howling, they would place their dead on pyres prepared for other men, apply the torches, maim and bleed and brawl to keep the corpses from abandonment.

Robotics is the third technology, and it's really different in the sense that the threat here is the creation of a wild successor species. Nanoelectronics seems to give us sufficient CPU power so that we could create something on the scale of a brain. The subsequent dangers have been broadly outlined by Hans Moravec in his book *Robot*.

Robots would be very different from us. They'd probably be asexual, Lamarckian—meaning that they could pass experience directly—and they wouldn't necessarily have a strong notion of an individual. So, any romantic notion that robots would be like people, I think, is a folly.

The most important thing to note about implementing robots is that it's a real change to the evolutionary paradigm. We had biological evolution until humans came along and, since then, evolution has been largely dominated by cultural evolution, which might go, say, a thousand times faster than biological evolution. The technological evolution is moving much, much faster than cultural evolution and perhaps a million times faster than biological evolution. It's no surprise that it's difficult for cultural institutions to maintain any sort of notion of control over the technology.

The danger with these technologies—GNR—is extremist and delusional people. Writing in the *Seattle Times* in response to my article in *Wired,* William Calvin, a neurobiologist at the University of Washington, wrote: "There's a class of people with delusional disorder who can remain employed and pretty functional for decades. Even if they're only one percent of the population, that's 25,000 mostly untreated, delusional people in the Puget Sound area. Even if only one percent of these has the intelligence or education to intentionally create sustained or widespread harm, it's still a pool of 200 high-performing, sociopathic or delusional techies in the Puget Sound area alone."

Now, the question really is: are we going to give the people in our society who are clearly crazy—and we can't deny that they're out there—illimitable power? Imagine that we're all on an airline together, the airplane being the planet, but on Egypt Airline 990 where everyone's a pilot and everyone has a button to crash the plane by doing one of these crazy things. That's clearly not acceptable—it brings back fate, like we saw in the ancient world. It's insane to create widespread enabling of genocide or extinction.

People have proposed technical fixes to this problem. Carl Sagan saw the problem and said, "Well, we could head to the stars." But I don't think there's enough time, and who would take ethical responsibility for the people who were left behind? Ray Kurzweil imagined we'd all become one with technology since we'd all upload ourselves into being robots, but the robots would certainly have their own psychological problems. If anything, given that they'd be smarter and more powerful than we are, that seems like an even more dangerous situation. The people who didn't choose to be robots would be in particular peril even if it were possible, which is arguable.

Other people have argued for shields. Luis Alvarez, a great physicist, said of the people who proposed the great SDI shield: "They were bright guys with no common sense." I think the reality is that the ability to create havoc with these technologies will probably out-race our ability to defend against them. That doesn't mean we shouldn't try to create some defenses, but a defense against any bioengineered pathogen would be the rough analogue of a perfect human immune system, which seems unlikely given that, for example, today we have no cures for any viral diseases.

> *The ability to create havoc with these technologies will probably out-race our ability to defend against them.*

So, in order to deal with this problem as we had to deal with the nuclear problem, we have to look beyond technical fixes to non-technical fixes. We could hope for a Second Coming, something faith-based. But if you talk to people of faith, you find out that God isn't going to come back to save us from ourselves in any major faith that I can find. In fact, we have the freedom to destroy ourselves—that's part of the covenant after the Noah and the Ark story in my faith. We are responsible for ourselves and what we have to do, I think, is decide how we're going to manage these technologies to reduce the danger. We have done some things along these lines. Historically, starting in the Nixon administration, for example, the U.S. renounced the use and research of offensive, biological weapons. The weapons of this category are so bad that you don't even want to make them, even if the enemy makes them, because the ones you are making might get stolen by somebody else. Since there's no defense, the only real answer is to not have them in the first place.

How much danger is there? John Leslie, the Canadian philosopher, estimated the danger of our extinction at roughly 30 percent, but much more if you accept something called the Doomsday argument. . . . Ray Kurzweil said, in his book *The Age of Spiritual*

Machines, meaning robots: "We have a better than even chance of making it through, but I've always been accused of being an optimist."

We have an ethical issue: if these technologies can cause genocide or extinction, and genocide is a crime of the highest possible order, we as scientists and technologists must not be complicit in genocide. We have to put in limits or safeguards on development. And it has to account for the reality of extremists.

We've got to move beyond fatalism; we don't want to risk our future on the fact that we'll be able somehow to come up with defenses for things that are almost impossible to defend against through some magical intervention of cleverness.

Now, the scientific attitude has always revered knowledge above all things. Robert Oppenheimer, two months after the bomb was dropped on Hiroshima, said: "It's not possible to be a scientist unless you believe that the knowledge of the world and the power that it gives is a thing that is of intrinsic value to humanity. And scientists [should be] using it to help spread knowledge and be willing to take the consequences"—essentially, disclaiming any responsibility as scientists for the further use of the things you're creating.

I agree that knowledge is good, and so is the search for truths. We clearly have a bedrock value in our society long agreed on—the value of open access to information and the problems that arise with attempts to restrict access to and the development of knowledge. Certainly, in recent times, we've come to particularly revere scientific knowledge. Yet, despite the strong historical precedents, if open access to and unlimited development of knowledge puts us all in clear danger of extinction, then common sense demands that we re-examine even the basic long held truths.

Nietzsche warned us at the end of the 19th century, not only that God was dead, but that "faith in science, which, after all, exists undeniably, cannot owe its origin to a calculus of utility. It must have originated, in spite of the fact that the disutility and dangerousness of the will to truth or truth at any price, is proved to it constantly." It's this further danger that we now fully face: the consequences of our truth seeking. The truth that science seeks can certainly be considered a dangerous substitute for God if it's likely to lead to our extinction.

Edith Hamilton, in *The Greek Way*, points out that "the wisest of Roman law-givers said that 'the enforcement of an absolutely just law, without any exceptions, irrespective of particular differences, worked absolute injustice.'" And so we see here that, even if the pursuit of truth and openness is an absolutely just thing, that even it must admit exceptions, such as in this case.

Aristotle, perhaps the founder of science, in his book on ethics pointed out that "the final end of human life is happiness, not truth." He said, "We call final without qualification that which is always desirable in itself and never for the sake of something else. Such a thing happiness, above all else, is because we never choose it for the sake of something else." The Dalai Lama has made a similar point in arguing for secular ethics in his book *Ethics for the New Millennium*. Both, in this way, clearly recognize the limits of science.

There's been a lot of reaction to the article I wrote. I've been very encouraged by people's willingness to engage this subject. The 20th century was clearly a bloody century, a century of war, a century of creation of enormously horrible weapons. We fortunately avoided nuclear disaster. We unfortunately created the ability for the nation states to destroy civilization. The 21st century may be a century of pestilence if we don't take some action, more like the 14th or, perhaps, the 16th century. I think we have to change our ways to avoid such disasters. We can't afford to democratize extreme evil.

I think we have to find a new way of thinking about the world, perhaps thinking of earth as a sanctuary for people. If our home is a sanctuary for our children, we don't leave loaded guns lying around the house. If the zoo is a sanctuary for animals, we don't take toxic chemicals and PCBs into the zoo. So, there are certainly things that we're clever enough to make that we shouldn't have on the earth, and that's the challenge that's in front of us.

Thank you.

Testimony before the State of California Advisory Committee on Human Cloning[3]

Glenn McGee

Assistant professor of bioethics, philosophy and history and sociology of science, University of Pennsylvania and its Center for Bioethics; B.A. in philosophy, Baylor University; Ph.D. in philosophy, Vanderbilt University; member, U.S. Food and Drug Administration Molecular and Genetic Devices Panel; senior research fellow, Kennedy Institute for Ethics, Georgetown University; associate, Ethics Institute, Dartmouth College; senior fellow, Leonard Davis Institute for Health Care Economics; chair, Ethics Advisory Board of Advanced Cell Technology; works with the Pew Charitable Trusts on program development in Bioethics; authored more than 100 articles and one book, Perfect Baby, 1997, 2nd edition, 2000; editor, Human Cloning Debate, 1998, and Pragmatic Bioethics, 1999; editor-in-chief, American Journal of Bioethics, and the Basic Bioethics book series, MIT Press; writes monthly column for MS-NBC Online; Atlantic Fellowship in Public Policy by the British government, 1999–2000.

Editors' introduction: In testimony in the Junipero Serra Building before the Advisory Committee on Human Cloning in California, sponsored by the Department of Health Services of California, Dr. Glenn McGee argued that "the strategy that makes the most sense morally, legally and perhaps even politically, is to identify and promote those features of existing law and policy that point to shared communal views about parenthood, while treating the problem of cloning not as a matter for Camelot-style top-down regulation but rather as a matter for public discussion and slow communal progress."

Glenn McGee's speech: Thank you for inviting me to advise the Committee concerning the extension of the California ban on human cloning. California is one of only three states to ban human cloning, and the disposition of this matter will be very important for my own state of Pennsylvania and for the nation. This is clearly a case in which the old truism about California leading the states will be true, whether for better or worse.

---

3. Delivered September 22, 2000, in Los Angeles, California, 1:30 p.m. Reprinted with permission of Glenn McGee.

I have been asked to answer two questions in my testimony this morning. First I will reflect on the question of whether there are moral or ethical considerations that would support a continued California ban on any therapeutic application of cloning, if safety and efficiency of cloning were not a problem? Second I will discuss the question of whether or not, in the absence of a ban, there are moral or ethical abuses that should be averted by regulations?

Biographical and Conflict of Interest Statement

I am a fellow in the Center for Bioethics at the University of Pennsylvania and an assistant professor of molecular and cellular engineering, philosophy, and history and sociology of science. I'm a philosopher by training with additional training in genetics. My research has been in the area of reproductive technology generally, with cloning and stem cell research as areas of specialization. My initial study of human cloning per se was a team effort with scientist Ian Wilmut, aimed at identifying morally defensible models for the regulation of human cloning research. I served as ethicist to the team that authored Rhode Island General Law #23-16.4 in 1998, a law banning the reproductive use of human cloning, a law which you may know is based only in part on that of California (in Rhode Island we defined cloning more specifically). In 1997 I worked with a public policy group in Brazil as it crafted cloning legislation, and this year I spent six months in London as an Atlantic Fellow in Public Policy of the United Kingdom, where I conducted a study of the relationship between U.S. and British policy on cloning and stem cell research. My research group has conducted a few qualitative and quantitative studies of the correlation between adult expectations of future offspring and the desire to use particular reproductive technologies. I have read and written broadly as a philosopher about the meaning of infertility. Finally, I have directed a course that requires students to learn to write state bioethics policy, which this past year involved the supervision of 35 University of Pennsylvania students, each of whom authored and submitted proposed human cloning legislation in their home states.

Like Dr. Cunningham, I am a member of the federal Food and Drug Administration panel on Molecular and Clinical Genetic Devices, which would have jurisdiction to review any proposal for therapeutic human somatic cell nuclear transfer studies if, as Secretary Shalala suggested in 1998, human cloning research is subject to automatic U.S. F.D.A. review of any research that carries a greater than minimal risk to human subjects. Obviously I do not speak for the panel or the F.D.A. I also do not speak for Penn's department of molecular and cellular engineering or its gene therapy institute, which has been fictitiously associated with cloning in *Wired* magazine. Although as you have identified, I am editor-in-chief of the *American Journal of Bioethics* I do not speak for the editorial board or publishers of that journal. I serve as a member of the ethics advisory board of Advanced Cell Technology, a stem cell research corporation that conducted somatic cell nuclear transfer experiments involving animal and human material, and have participated in discussions of stem cell research held by Patient's CURe, an coalition of patient advocacy groups who support stem cell research. For both of these activities I have been compensated for travel alone. My comments in those contexts and in this one are strictly my own and I want to make clear that in no capacity do I have any conflict of interest in the matter of reproductive cloning arising from my relationship with any organization, political party or corporation.

Ethics Apart from Safety

Safety concerns have informed all existing legislation on human cloning. Safety concerns are often contrasted with ethical concerns, which is a difficult contrast to make. This is true not only because all of these safety questions present a matter of ethical importance, but also because virtually all the moral issues about human cloning amount to concerns for the welfare of children. I will not distinguish safety from ethics. My focus will be on the moral issues that remain even if human somatic cell nuclear transfer can be performed without greater than average risks of worse than average incidence of miscarriage or birth defects. I would contend that significant issues remain, and that these issues are an appropriate subject for state self-governance. However I do not believe that the present ban is appropriate.

> *It has been exhaustively argued in a number of contexts that human cloning may be oppressive to offspring.*

It has been exhaustively argued in a number of contexts that human cloning may be oppressive to offspring. Cloned human children would be unable to avoid many of the physical traits of a single specific person. As Arthur Caplan noted, a child whose parent is also the whole-genome donor would not only see the traits he or she would embody, but also see how many life processes are likely to play out. The challenges of cloning would face a parent-donor too, as he or she will be unable to wonder about the appearance of his or her child, and all to able to see in the child the lost youth of the parent. We have stories like "the birds and the bees" exactly to explain to our kids and ourselves what it means to make a child, and how intimacy is linked to heredity and parenthood. Parents of cloned children will have to make their children's "stories" up from scratch, and will not be able to draw on the wisdom or experience of parents for help. However one frames nuclear transfer, it is clearly an experiment with an entirely new kind of family.

The foundation for how governments should distinguish between normal and oppressive parenthood has been advanced by Joel Feinberg and reiterated by Dena Davis and many others: children have a "right to an open future." Feinberg says that children not only need to determine their own identity, they in fact have a right to do so. This right is understood as a "negative" right, preventing others from doing a harmful thing, rather than a positive right. A child has a positive right to vaccinations, and an even stronger right to food, and it could be argued that children's right to education (not itself constitutional in scope) is evidence of a positive right to an open future. But no scholar has gone beyond simple terms in arguing for a child's negative right to be free from parental interference in finding and choose an identity. I have argued that a child's negative right against loss of identity is encoded only tangentially in laws that regulate specific behaviors, for example parents are forbidden in all the U.S. states and territory from marrying or having sexual relationships with children. Parents who violate these laws see the harm quantified in terms of the future of the child. Likewise a parent who forced a child to act as an adult family member, insisting that the child work full-time to support the family, would in most states be subject to prosecution not only for neglect but also for violating rules about child labor that are designed to protect against robbing a child of its future by exploiting it during the time of childhood development. But these are extraordinary sorts of parental abuses. It is difficult to define an open future except unless one contrasts that opaque idea against some eggregious violation of a child's interest in future liberty.

Proponents of human cloning (and there are not many, nor do the most vocal proponents represent the arguments or existence of any sort of groundswell in demand for human cloning) have advanced very imaginative arguments. The simplest is the hardest to refute. The claim is that cloning is the same sort of thing as private schools, expensive vitamins, orthodontics, and other enhancements available to children. Many children today are essentially stylized to become particular sorts of children or adults. It is evident in the 27th Olympic games as one watches an veritable army of 12 year-old gymnasts with multiple prior bone injuries. Perhaps the Olympics best demonstrate how significant is the role of parental goals for children in the American dream. Every western child named Jr. can tell a story about how that form of parental thinking about the sharing of identity across generations has affected his identity and self-perception. Proponents of cloning thus point to the extensive protections of procreative liberty as well as the economic stratification of institutions that provide for the future of children. Wealthier parents can secure surrogate mothers, pay extra for smart sperm donors, make their children more attractive, teach them to succeed on standardized tests through expensive prep courses and even improve their kids adolescent adjustment through pharmacology. It is difficult, proponents argue, to see why cloning is a special case of infraction of the "open future" principle, or to see why cloning must have special rules.

It seems to me that this entire argument misses the point. It is a mistake to legislate a child's special right to an open future when so much of parenting is exactly about guiding children by providing them with, and indeed insisting that they accept, a considerable number of moral premises. No pediatrician would contest the fact that a parent who refuses to teach a child right from wrong is guilty of neglect. Elevating the diverse responsibilities of parents to the status of a simple right of children to have a fully "open" future is probably unconstitutional. But I am not a scholar of constitutional law. I only want to argue that the "open future" claim is unnecessary and confusing, and that the effort to use "open future" as a way of protecting potential future generations against cloning is motivated by a need to find some single universal moral rule to prevent cloning. In part the public and lawmakers want a single simple rule to enable national and international consensus, so that people cannot "go offshore," or even to Nevada, for cloning. It seems to me that the moral precepts that matter about cloning have to be discussed and finally regulated in the murky water of state law, alongside the majority of administrative and case law about reproduction, children, and pediatrics. At that level it is possible to discuss the matter of cloning not in terms of protecting a child's open future, but rather to frame the question in terms of what sort of thing reproductive cloning is and should be, alongside other similar problems that are regulated and discussed in smaller moral communities than the U.S. Congress.

Understood in terms of a child's right to an open future, there is a profound metaphysical problem—and there is indeed no other way to describe it—of whether or not a future child, whose embryonic origins have not even begun, has any rights; many philosophers worry about the so-called Parfit's problem, the upshot of which is that a child can be harmed by existence only if that child would be better off not having been created. I will not rehearse these problems. As Ian Wilmut and I argue, the problem is not so much about a child's right to be his or her own person as it is about states' responsibility to regulate many aspects of the family. Wilmut and I have identified as one example of such state regulation the rules governing adoption. In every state but Oregon, couples who wish to adopt a child are both aided and restricted by laws. These laws identify, protect, and acknowledge each member of a prospective adoptive family. Adoption laws are an important precedent for cloning law, demonstrating the role that the state is supposed to play. It is often asserted that procreative freedom—the negative right against state interference in couples' choices about having children—extends to all kinds of reproductive technology. In the face of states' respect for reproductive freedom, states overtly restrict adoption. Why? For exactly the reasons I have intimated. It is a mistake to reduce these multiple interests of the state to "a child's right to an open future." In fact they are tied to many interests of future generations, along with interests of the parents and their community. Adoption law is a positive as well as restrictive force, aimed at aiding the development of responsible parenting

---

The problem is not so much about a child's right to be his or her own person as it is about states' responsibility to regulate many aspects of the family.

---

where there is both evidence of potential problems and a clear need for support. An enormous advantage of adoption law, one which suggests that adoption might be a viable model for the regulation of human cloning, is that adoption law draws on the wisdom of communal governance. It is important to note that in California, family court judges are invariably the jurists to rule on matters such as harvesting and use of sperm from the dead, surrogacy contracts, divorce involving frozen embryos and other reproductive technologies that result in litigation. Whether or not one chooses to regulate cloning through the family courts, it will find its way there eventually.

There are significant moral issues involved in human cloning, including the nest of problems that have been identified by the "open future" advocates as well as those Mark Eibert and others point to about reproductive freedom. But there is little promise in a debate about liberties of children and hopeful parents. The best hope is that a responsible regulatory framework can come out of state efforts to reconstruct existing laws. These efforts should not be guided by the compelling but bizarre cases and aspects of human somatic cell nuclear transfer. Rather the strategy that makes the most sense morally, legally and perhaps even politically, is to identify and promote those features of existing law and policy that point to shared communal views about parenthood, while treating the problem of cloning not as a matter for Camelot-style top-down regulation but rather as a matter for public discussion and slow communal progress. The present ban should be allowed to expire. It should be replaced by an act requiring every family court judge in the state to initiate develop and promulgate regulations about new reproductive technologies involving somatic cell nuclear transfer. These rules should be couched at the state level in a set of basic guidelines, developed by this group, about what sort of thing cloning is.

I am a pragmatist with regard to the sorts of principles that should be involved or their origins in religion or ultimate truth. In my view such matters must be discussed and resolved strictly within the context where they have meaning, and the goal of all law that deals with sensitive moral matters should be to protect as much as possible the capacity of human beings to flourish in many innovative ways that respond to the diversity of California's communities.

Ethical Abuses to be Avoided by Regulation

The debate about whether and how to extend restrictions on human cloning is not aimed at the sort of program I propose. Simple hearings of this kind are not going to identify the bodies of relevant law in California, nor is the present group ideal to write legislation. It is also notable that there is almost no funding at all for research into the dangers and scope of reproductive technology. I am supposing from the budget and mandate given to this committee that your purpose of this group is to decide whether or not to continue the ban on cloning, not to rethink how the debate about cloning should be integrated into California's institutions. And I must say that this is unfortunate and avoidable, particularly in a state as innovative as this one. I would plead that before you make recommendations you commission at least some studies aimed at determining what sorts of pitfalls have been encountered by new parents who have used other highly unusual reproductive technologies. However within the context of whether or not to renew the law I do have a few comments about how regulations can avoid needless ethical abuses.

First, cloning must be clearly defined, and I would further suggest that the term cloning itself must be replaced by nuclear-transfer derived offspring. The matter of stem cell research is entirely separate, unless one wants to consider the ways in which stem cell research advance the basic science that would be needed prior to a safe attempt at human cloning. Cloning is altering biologists' descriptions of an embryo and altering clinicians' ideas about viability. Ironically, much more research into the processes that take place when enucleated oocytes are jarred into developing as embryos after the transfer of a nucleas from a somatic cell will be required before there is any stability in the world where embryos, totipotency, and cloning are defined. So any definition must allow room for the arbitrariness of the present state of terminology about development.

Second, the fear of offshore cloning must be attacked. This fear is unfounded from my perspective, since California can enforce its rules about marriage, divorce, adoption and cloning in ways that would prevent patients from going out of state to seek services ille-

---

> ## *The dangers and goals in new reproductive technology are . . . merely more profound forms of the good and bad goals that parents already have.*

---

gal in their district. California will very likely be the first state to adopt real rules that go beyond a simple ban on cloning, and it is the purview of California to worry about those who live elsewhere and have children there in ways Californians find reprehensible. Already there are at least 10 reproductive acts that my group identified as legal in West Virginia that would be illegal for adults in Los Angeles.

The practice of human nuclear transfer may allow many individuals and couples who would otherwise be forced to adopt, and thus be unable to transmit their hereditary information to the next generation. At the same time, it is exactly this powerful desire to transmit genetic information that frightens those who want children to have an "open future." Somewhere in the middle is the truth: the dangers and goals in new reproductive technology are not special or new. They are merely more profound forms of the good and bad goals that parents already have. I worked to help Rhode Island because in my view a short-term ban of cloning on simple safety grounds was justified. But with the possibility of safe cloning on the horizon, the debate must now shift to the real issues about how to modulate public education and debate. My hope for you is that you choose diligent research and consultation with the seasoned institutions of California law rather than the inviting, but ultimately unsuccessful, Camelot-style of ethics in public policy "from on high."

VI. International Issues

Foreign Policy Priorities for a New Century[1]

Lamar Alexander

Chairman, the Nashville, TN, Salvation Army Initiative, to help families move from welfare to work; chairman and co-founder, Simplexis, which helps schools with their purchases; born Maryville, TN, July 3, 1940, B.A. (Phi Beta Kappa), Vanderbilt University, 1962; J.D. (Law review editor), New York University Law School, 1965; co-founder and partner, Dearborn & Ewing Law Firm, 1970–76; governor of Tennessee, 1979–87; chairman, National Governor's Association 1985–86; chairman, Southern Regional Education Board; president of the University of Tennessee, 1988–91; U.S. Education Secretary, 1991–93; candidate for the Republican nomination for president of the United States, 1996 and 2000; author of New Promise of American Life, *1994,* We Know What To Do, *1995, and* Lamar Alexander's Little Plaid Book, *1995.*

Editors' introduction: Former Governor Lamar Alexander spoke at the American Enterprise Institute to 300 invited guests. This was one of six major policy addresses delivered during the 2000 presidential campaign. Mr. Alexander describes this speech as outlining "the principles and priorities I believe should guide U.S. foreign policy in the next century." Concerned that the U.S. armed forces "do more with fewer resources," Governor Alexander advised the nation's leaders "to be selective about our missions," which should satisfy three criteria: "credibility, the willingness to lead, and a strategic vision."

Lamar Alexander's speech: Nearly a decade ago, the Cold War came to an end with the collapse of the Soviet Union and communism. At the time, you could almost hear the collective sigh of relief of the American people—from coast to coast.

But the post–Cold War world has turned out to be more dangerous and complex than many Americans expected. It has not been possible to relegate foreign affairs to reduced status. For me this fact was reinforced recently when I met with a number of leaders in Western Europe and Russia.

---

1. Delivered in Washington, D.C., on February 11, 1999, in the evening. Reprinted with permission of Lamar Alexander.

In these post–Cold War years change has been the one constant. Country after country adopted the forms of democratic capitalism, but some have not understood how its content must work to improve the lives of ordinary people—not just a few people who could get very rich in a short period.

Who would have thought, a decade ago, that the threat of hundreds of Soviet missiles raining down on us would be replaced by the threat of one missile targeted on one U.S. city by a rogue state, or deadly viruses or poison gas smuggled here in a suitcase?

These threats have become real, and we can only imagine how much worse they would have been if the United States, as the one remaining superpower, had not stood in the way. Yet, our government is still having difficulty adjusting to that new reality of being the world's only superpower, as reflected in its ambivalence toward the projection of American power in the pursuit of vital national interests.

> *Our government is still having difficulty adjusting to that new reality of being the world's only superpower.*

The well-known American impulse for generosity led us to a failed commitment of military resources to so-called "nation-building" in Somalia. We sent a task force to Haiti, ostensibly to help the people there create a democratic framework from which to create prosperity, but today the people of Haiti are just as poor and exploited as ever.

In the former Yugoslavia, we and some of our European allies are trying to impose a multiethnic society where one never existed. We sent our troops to Bosnia to help stop aggression. In step with the political correctness of the day, our government was obsessed from the outset with a so-called "exit strategy," when a *"success strategy"* should have been our first priority. And how can we ever succeed when we blur the basic difference between victim and aggressor?

The "exit strategy" was to have our troops home within a year. That was three years ago. They are still mired there. We still do not have a definition of "success" for the region—only vague concepts of it. Once our troops do come home, who doubts that fighting will break out again?

In Kosovo, endless talk with Serbia's dictator, Slobodan Milosevic, has produced nothing but broken promises. Once again, NATO is threatening to take action, including putting troops there as "peacekeepers." If our allies want to send in troops, fine. Our role should be to give them logistical and air support. This time, "no American boots on the ground."

Today, we have members of our armed forces in some eighty countries around the world. At the same time, our national defense budget—as a percentage of our gross domestic product—is lower than it was at the end of World War II. In short, we are asking our armed services to do more with fewer resources.

We need to be selective about our missions. When we act, we must be decisive *and* committed to a clear standard of success. And, our troops must have nothing less than the very best training and equipment our nation can provide.

No one ever said it would be easy being the world's only super-power and its principal exponent of democratic capitalism. While we may not always feel comfortable in this role, it is ours and will be for quite some time to come.

A common phrase is that "We cannot be the world's policeman." While it is true we cannot be the cop on every corner, it is also true that if we were not "on the beat" in some of the world's high crime areas, no one else would be. And, if we don't continue going into those areas, sooner or later the high crimes will be in our neighborhood.

To set forth our foreign policy priorities for a new century we must meet three basic requirements:

- Credibility;
- The willingness to lead, and . . .
- A strategic vision.

Having credibility means that what we say will be believed. When we are credible, potential adversaries will fear us and friends and allies respect us. It also means conferring with those friends and allies before we issue threats to adversaries. What it does *not* mean is making repeated threats of action then backing off, as we did repeatedly with Iraq and not long ago with Serbia's offensive in Kosovo.

You'll recall that NATO planes streamed across the Serbian sky, symbolizing the danger Milosevic faced if he did not comply with a deadline to pull his forces out of Kosovo. At the last minute, he said he needed another ten days to withdraw. Our reply was, "Okay." He is still not complying and we are once again threatening air strikes. Will it turn out once again to be bluster?

George Shultz once told me that Ronald Reagan's most successful foreign policy initiative was when he fired the striking air traffic controllers. You'll recall that they threatened to strike. President Reagan said that if they didn't return to work within a specified period of time, they would be terminated. They struck and he fired them. George Shultz told me, "As Secretary of State, it made my job a lot easier. Every foreign leader I dealt with knew we had a president who would do what he said he would do." It's still true that we build credibility by saying what we mean and meaning what we say.

There are occasions for studied ambiguity, as in the case of China and Taiwan. For years we have insisted that the possible reunification of these two Chinese societies is a matter for them to determine—by peaceful means. Taiwan says this can only happen when the mainland becomes a democratic society. The Communists, meanwhile, pursue their strategy of trying to isolate Taiwan internationally.

On his trip to China last year, President Clinton weakened our position of studied ambiguity—a position developed by administrations of both parties—when he enunciated and thus endorsed the Communists' three "nos." These are: No support for an independent Taiwan; No "one China, one Taiwan;" and no membership for Taiwan in any international organization requiring statehood. Mr. Clinton went well beyond anything his predecessors had said. It was unnecessary and appeared to tilt the playing field, something we had assiduously avoided since 1979 when we first extended diplomatic recognition to Beijing.

Our credibility is perishable, but our responsibilities are not. One of these responsibilities has been to lead the Western alliance for half a century. NATO has been a remarkable success. It held the Soviet threat in check while the countries of Western Europe built prosperous economies.

Now, NATO has expanded to include the Czech Republic, Hungary and Poland. Others in the former Soviet bloc are anxious to be included in the alliance. The door is open. Further NATO expansion must be handled with great care, partly because of the cost of expansion, partly because of NATO's relationship with Russia, and partly because the time has come to rethink NATO's mission and redefine it for a new century.

Our goal remains a Europe that is whole, free, prosperous and secure. Toward that end, I believe we should energetically explore the idea of a transatlantic free-trade area; an economic arrangement that would reach out to new and potential allies in Central and Eastern Europe, while opening fresh possibilities for American companies and their products. This is an initiative that could strengthen our ties with friends on the western half of the continent and, once and for all, make transatlantic trade wars a thing of the past.

NATO was created and maintained for the purpose of checking Soviet ambitions toward Western Europe. Today, that threat is gone, but it has been replaced by new threats, such as regional ethnic wars, terrorism and rogue states in possession of weapons of mass destruction. In Bosnia, NATO—with the U.S. taking the lead—initially went in to perform the new role of separating warring groups. In Kosovo, two NATO members, France and Germany, went further. Of the 1,600 NATO troops in the so-called Extraction Force, France offered 800 and Germany 200.

A recent joint declaration by British Prime Minister Blair and French President Chirac signaled a move toward a European command structure within NATO. This is another instance of our European partners taking on wider responsibilities for regional security. Some Americans worry about what they see is growing divergence from the U.S. I see it as a healthy sign.

While we nurture the mutually indispensable transatlantic link,

---

While we nurture the mutually indispensable transatlantic link, we should welcome the assertion of European integration, not view it negatively.

---

we should welcome the assertion of European integration, not view it negatively. How often have we heard that "it's about time the Europeans take responsibility for their own security?" I think we should see their steps in that direction as a positive sign, not as a challenge to our leadership or our national objectives.

There are two reasons for this. One is our lead in productivity. Our rate keeps growing and is ahead of that of any of our European partners. The other reason is that Europe faces some real challenges. Bureaucracy and entitlements that are far beyond those in this country are embedded in the laws of Germany, France and other Western European countries. These act as a drag on venture capital and a brake on the creation of new jobs. Despite bold talk by left-leaning European governments that they will lower their countries' high unemployment rates, don't bet on it.

The EU nations will do what they can to solve their problems. What we can do to be better partners with them in the Western alliance is to confer with them before we act. In my meetings in Bonn, Paris and London, there were frequent calls for greater consultation—not calls for veto power on American action, but rather a wish not to be blind-sided—and especially not for domestic political reasons in the United States. One senior French leader put it succinctly when he said, "Cooperation and consultations between us were never better than during Desert Storm." We took the lead, but brought our allies in on our thinking and planning.

This April, NATO will mark its 50th anniversary with a major conference in Washington. This presents an important opportunity for reflection, as well as for new ideas about NATO's role in the next century. As a force comprised of peace-loving nations either fully democratic or in active transition to that status, NATO could become a troubleshooting organization to answer the threats of terrorists and rogue states both inside and outside its area. And, European states should recognize the stake they have in out-of-area threats.

With history in mind, some of Russia's neighbors view it as a potential threat; hence their desire to join NATO. When you talk with a variety of Russian leaders, however, as I did in Moscow, you a get a rather different perspective about NATO. Their line of reasoning is that NATO, after all, was formed as a bulwark against the Soviet Union. Now, if it expands to include the Baltic states and other immediate neighbors of Russia—but not Russia—should it not be seen as having hostile intentions toward Russia? You and I know that is not the case, but we need to explain it—often—to the Russians.

The time may come when NATO, with a revised mission, will consider inviting Russia to join, rather than having it standing to one side in the so-called "Partnership for Peace." Meanwhile, when Russia and NATO have common interests—such as thwarting terrorism—we should make common cause. Gradually, this process can help reduce old anxieties—both east and west.

This recent trip was my first to Russia in twelve years. In Moscow I was again struck by the evidence of personal freedom. People come and go as they wish. Wide boulevards, once almost devoid of vehicles, now have rush-hour traffic jams. There are attractive new stores. Newspapers and television news shows flourish. And, the variety and patronage of cultural events is impressive.

It is said that if Russia has a success story, it is Moscow, yet misery characterizes life in many other parts of the country. Nevertheless, progress is being made. Boris Nemtsov, a dynamic former provincial governor and First Deputy Prime Minister last year, tells of the important beginnings of federalism under President Yeltsin—a shift from a completely centralized economy controlled from Moscow. Governors are now elected and half the taxes collected at the local and provincial level stay there instead of going to Moscow.

Historically, the Russian people have shown great strength and stoicism in the face of adversity. A new round of it began last August. The government defaulted on bonds sold to foreign investors. Domestically, this was a case of too few rubles chasing too many entitlements. The government was paying these entitlements with borrowed money. It finally ran out of cash to redeem its bonds.

The currency was devalued, followed by money-printing. Prime Minister Primakov said he would continue to print money to meet basic needs. If he does, it is a recipe for trouble.

The Primakov government has submitted a budget that would be balanced were it not for foreign loans to be repaid. He will need a restructuring of loans in order to keep it balanced. Meanwhile, lenders see a country with serious corruption in government; insider privatization sales; fortunes made by a few, but prosperity spread not nearly as wide as it must be to build a vigorous middle class. These problems are aggravated by capital flight.

Russia's over-borrowing has caused serious problems and, with it, a setback for basic reforms. In the near term we may see some protectionist trade measures, renationalization of some privatized industries and other seemingly regressive moves.

Given all this, some say, forget about Russia; we have less trade with them than with the Dominican Republic. While that is true, Russia is a huge country and its stability involves our own vital national interests.

One success story in our relationship with Russia is the Nunn-Lugar program, by which we provide approximately $400 million a year and technical experts to help the Russians dismantle nuclear weapons and safely store the resulting fissionable material.

The Russian leaders I met with represent a variety of constituencies and views. I heard much pessimism, but also hope that the future will be better if new ideas are brought to bear. Russia still lacks private land ownership. It is said that the city of Moscow is considering selling some municipal property to private owners this year in a pilot program.

One leader told me that, in addition to the need for private land ownership, Russia needs a sound, fully trustworthy judicial system and a civil society, in the sense we in the West understand that term.

All of these leaders are seeking a new definition of Russia's role in the world. There are differing approaches. Some see a westward-orientation—to Europe, NATO and the United States. Others talk of a concept they call "Eurasia," in which Russia becomes the linch-pin of a new power equation. The recent overtures by the Russian government to China and India for a tripartite relationship are a symptom of this. So is the proposed union of Russia and Belarus.

Still others see the "Eurasia" idea as primarily a bridge of commerce between Europe, Asia and North America. For example, Alexander Lebed, the former general and now governor of Russia's largest province, talks of "Eurasia" in terms of an air bridge between Alaska and Siberia by which thousands of cargo flights a year could reduce shipping time of goods between North America and Europe. Among other things, this would require a significant improvement in Russia's air traffic control system.

One leader said to me that the United States lacks a post–Cold War strategy toward Russia, yet he added that the Europeans and Japan will do nothing without U.S. participation. Thus, it is U.S. *leadership* that is essential.

We can do a better job of understanding the Russians. Theirs is a major country deserving of respect, despite the difficult times they are going through. Indeed, our strategy for U.S.–Russian relations

---

It is in our interest that Russia be an economically strong friend rather than a weak and truculent competitor.

---

must flow from recognition of the fact that *it is in our interest that Russia be an economically strong friend rather than a weak and truculent competitor.* There are a number of areas where Russian and U.S. interests coincide. For example, controlling the spread of nuclear weapons, guarding against terrorism, maintaining the safety of nuclear power plants, combating drug trade and fighting organized crime. And, it is important to remember that, as long as Russians aspire to have a full democracy with a market economy, the genie that Gorbachev let out of the bottle more than a decade ago won't go back in.

In the Middle East, the Palestinian–Israeli peace process is on "hold" until Israel holds elections. Meanwhile, a positive action was the PLO's recent recantation of elements of its charter calling for the destruction of Israel.

A step backward would be a unilateral declaration of Palestinian statehood by Yassar Arafat on May 4. That is an issue that must be left for the final status talks. Chairman Arafat should be applauded for his renunciation of terror in recent years. It makes peace possible. But we must continue to stand by our democratic ally Israel, and continue to insist that Palestinians accept the position that violence must now and forever become a political tool of the past. Only this can make peace a lasting reality. The death of King Hussein silences an important voice for peace in the region. The example of his statesmanship should continue to serve as an inspiration to both sides—that past animosities *can* be laid aside if one looks ahead instead of through a rear-view mirror.

As for Iraq, it is high time the United States makes its objective the removal of Saddam Hussein from power, to be replaced by a democratic government. If we're serious, this objective requires a clear strategy. I recommend the following steps: Identify and back a government in exile. Then, openly support that government. Meanwhile, continue steady enforcement of the "no-fly" zones. Fourth, provide humanitarian aid for Saddam's endangered opponents in the north and south.

In Africa, several countries are in turmoil. Regional efforts are made to quell this and our focus should be on encouraging investment where it has a good chance of producing results. Ghana and Botswana come to mind. And, of course, South Africa, despite problems of increased crime, still has the potential for being the economic engine that can pull many of its neighbors forward. Throughout the sub-Saharan Africa there continues to be a great need for medicines, vaccines and technology for pure water supplies.

In Asia, American leadership has gone off course. Japan—the world's second largest economy—is Asia's economic engine. It is in everyone's interest—especially ours—to see that Japan comes out of its slump. The Japanese are very slow to make fundamental changes, but the government of Prime Minister Obuchi appears finally to be coming to grips with the crisis of Japan's hide-bound banking system and the need for substantial tax cuts.

It has not helped that for months U.S. officials badgered and scapegoated the Japanese. President Clinton's failure to visit Japan after his China trip last year—a curious concession to Chinese demands—was seen as a snub. Months later he made a quick visit to Tokyo, but damage had already been done to Japanese confidence in U.S. commitments to the region.

The situation has been aggravated by two other developments. One involved the nuclear tests by India and Pakistan and the missile firing by North Korea. This drew a great deal of U.S. attention away from the Japan relationship. The other development was Mr. Clinton's unrestrained embrace of the Chinese leadership.

This gave rise to Japanese concerns that the U.S. intends to play China off against Japan for the purpose of wringing trade concessions from the Japanese. While this may not have been the motive behind the Clinton trip to China, it demonstrated that the administration is not sensitive to the thinking of our most important ally in Asia. I can tell you from my days as Governor, when I went to Japan often to negotiate auto plants for our state, that every word and action has a meaning.

While China can neither be ignored nor expected to do just as we wish, it is not our ally in any sense of the word. Nor can China provide meaningful investment capital to other nations in the region. Japan is that provider. China *does* have the potentiality for becoming a major military power. This frightens its neighbors, especially the Japanese. The Chinese have been relentless in their quest for technology that will give them military hegemony in the region. And, as we learned from elements of a Congressional select committee's investigative report, the transfer of American satellite technology to China has compromised our national security.

Nowadays, almost any store you visit will be filled with products marked "Made in China." The stores like these products because they can be competitively priced and the profit margins are high. But the downside is a lopsided trade imbalance. Last year, we imported $202 billion-worth of goods from China, but exported only $90 billion. It is said that the Chinese government considers an eight percent annual growth rate as essential to keep civil peace. Whatever their growth target, economically the Chinese need us much more than we need them. We should not forget that.

While China can neither be ignored nor expected to do just as we wish, it is not our ally in any sense of the word.

Then there is the matter of human rights. Beijing treats any efforts at democratization as subversion and takes the position that it is none of our business. That simply does not wash. The Chinese on Taiwan are proof of that. They achieved the world's first democratic Chinese society by replacing authoritarianism with a vigorous, multi-party democracy. There, everybody is free to express any opinion he or she wishes. Even the phrase "independence for Taiwan" won't land anyone in jail.

But, on the mainland, they insist on a single-party, and free speech is anathema. Recently, four dissidents were given long prison sentences for advocating such shocking things as forming a political party and a labor union. So much for Mr. Clinton's talk-show gimmickry in Shanghai and his embrace of China as some sort of evolving democracy.

We cannot ignore China, but there is no reason to get cozy with it either. If and when they improve their human rights conditions, we should encourage them. Meanwhile, we should trade with them, but we should remember that they will always act in what they consider to be *their* interest. We must do the same.

Here in our own hemisphere, an obvious example of U.S. leadership is the outpouring of help—public and private—for the countries of Central America that were devastated by Hurricane Mitch. A massive rebuilding program is in order, and we should lead the way in making it happen. In Brazil, we must hope that the IMF's efforts to stabilize the economy succeed. If they don't, there will be a big price to pay. Already, our steel makers and soybean farmers are feeling the competitive effects of Brazil's currency devaluation.

In these remarks, I have looked at American leadership from several angles and in several areas of the world. We have an administration whose successes and failures we can measure. Overall, it has reacted to events rather than anticipated and steered them. This may be due in part to a desire to get intelligence information that only reinforces its suppositions rather than challenges them. The administration seems to have an aversion to getting information that might cause it to make decisions it would rather defer (or hope would go away if ignored).

But this administration is in its final two years. What should be our vision for a new global strategy in a new century? I believe it should have three main elements: One is military strength and national security geared to future threats. Another is free and open trade. A third is support for and expansion of democratic movements wherever they are.

Regarding military strength and national security, two aspects are required. One is the ability to project military strength anywhere in the world rapidly and effectively. Our armed forces do a remarkably good job of this when you consider that the Clinton administration has let military spending—in constant dollars—slip to its lowest point since just after World War II. Equipment is either wearing out or becoming obsolescent much faster than the defense budget allows for its replacement. Mr. Clinton's call for increased defense spending does little to change this situation. Furthermore, he advocated military pay raises only after the problem of personnel retention had become a crisis.

If we are going to police hot spots, our armed forces need to be properly paid and they must have the best possible equipment. The appropriations and procurement processes are long and slow. The time to start a program of rebuilding is *now*.

Along with the ability to project our forces is the need for an actual defense of our nation against attack. We no longer think in terms of a cloud of Soviet nuclear warheads raining down on us. Our concern now is about the terrorist with the suitcase carrying vials of Sarin or biological agents or a nuclear device. Our concern must be also for the rogue state, desperate to draw its people's attention away from domestic disasters by aiming a missile at one of our cities.

For the suitcase-carrying terrorist, we need more effective screening procedures at our points of entry. And, we need better coordination of training of emergency personnel who would have to deal with biological or chemical attacks.

We need a missile defense system, as well. The upgraded theater-version of the Navy's Aegis system, which is expected to be operational within about two years, should become a building block for a national missile defense.

We know from last summer's Rumsfeld Commission report that we cannot expect to have the luxury of several years' warning before a rogue state is in a position to blackmail us with a weapon of mass destruction. Yet, W. Clinton does not plan to decide before next year whether to build a system by the year 2003. This year—now—is the time to make that commitment.

> *We must rededicate ourselves to the spread of representative democracy in every corner of the globe.*

The Clinton Administration is obsessed with the outdated ABM treaty. It has been amended before and will probably have to be amended again to accommodate this strategy. If this cannot be accomplished, we must be prepared to withdraw from it, while making it clear to the Russians that our missile defense is not intended to protect us against them, but against the new type of threat I have described.

We must move ahead on the trade front. We have become an exporting nation and that fact will not change. To improve our ability to engage in trade, the president needs so-called fast-track authority. This simply means that our negotiators will have the ability to complete agreements with trading partners without coming back to Congress to approve it a paragraph at a time. Presidents of both parties have had such authority for years, but in the last two years members of the president's own party have been holding it up, bowing to union and other protectionist pressures.

Along with making trade as free as possible between nations, we must have a moral component to our vision. We must rededicate ourselves to the spread of representative democracy in every corner of the globe.

As communism collapsed, many formerly one-party states adopted the forms but not the substance or spirit of multi-party representative democracy. Old habits die hard. In many of those countries government workers were underpaid; hence, bribes and corruption were common. In many there was little faith in the honesty or efficiency of government; therefore, tax-paying was ignored. We know from the American experience that honest government and tax compliance go hand-in-hand.

We must use every means at our disposal to help countries that are going through this transition. Investment is one way. Another is encouraging private and semi-public organizations that teach democratic political and economic principles to expand their work. Democratic capitalism, with its self-restraints and its checks and balances has brought the greatest prosperity to the largest number of people of any system yet devised. We must demonstrate its benefits every day and we must show them to the world.

It has been said that this century—the 20th—has been The American Century. Perhaps so, but I've got my eyes on the next one and I think the 21st can be another-American Century. America is a land that is never finished, but always beginning anew. That is why so many people aspire to what we have. We are the world's only superpower, and we should act it. That means setting objectives, communicating them, and carrying out plans to achieve them. In short, we should lead the world willingly, not reluctantly. The world will be richer for it.

On Permanent Normal Trade Relations with China[2]

John J. Lafalce

Representative from New York (D), U.S. House of Representatives, 1975– ; born Buffalo, NY, October 6, 1939; B.S., Canisius College, 1961; J.D., Villanova University School of Law, 1964; law clerk, Department of the Navy, Office of General Counsel, 1963; law lecturer, George Washington University, 1965–66; U.S. Army Adjutant General Corps (captain), 1965–67; Jaeckle, Fleischman and Mugel law firm, 1967–69; senator (D), New York State Legislature, 1971–72; assemblyman, New York State Legislature, 1973–74; Committee on Small Business, and Committee on Banking and Financial Services, U.S. Congress, 1974– ; has received several honorary law degrees from U.S. colleges and universities.

Editors' introduction: Participating in an extended debate in the U.S. Congress, Representative John J. LaFalce delivered an abbreviated form of this address in support of legislation granting Permanent Normal Trade Relations (PNTR) to China. Congressman LaFalce argued that the vote on this legislation would have far-reaching impact upon both economies and security internationally. Equally important, he contended, "influencing human rights in another country can be done far more effectively through engagement than through isolation." PNTR was approved by the Congress.

John J. Lafalce's speech: Mr. Speaker, the vote this week on whether to establish Permanent Normal Trade Relations (PNTR) with China will undoubtedly be the most important one we will take in this first year of the new millennium. I rise today to express my intent to vote "yes" on granting stable trade status to China and to explain, in some detail, the reasons behind my decision.

This issue involves the economies of the United States and China, and indeed the economies of nations around the world. But the judgments to be made involve far more than economic concerns alone. What we do this week will affect national and international security. It will set the agenda for how the U.S. interacts with China on such important matters as human and worker rights, the environ-

---

2. Delivered in the House of Representatives on May 24, 2000, published in its entirety in the *Congressional Record* of that date. Reprinted with permission of John LaFalce.

ment, and religious freedom. And it will help to determine how both the U.S. and China address the rest of the world for decades to come.

Evolution in China

Over the last two decades, I have been fortunate to witness the social and economic evolution in China "up close and personal." In January 1979, I traveled to Beijing as part of a Congressional delegation representing the United States as we reestablished diplomatic relations with China. This past week I reminisced with President Carter about that historic day, the intervening twenty years, and today's historic vote. We share virtually identical views.

Twenty years ago China was a backward, drab country just starting to recover from the disaster that Mao called "the Cultural Revolution." The streets were crowded—with pedestrians and bicycles. A few newspapers posted on a few walls were the only visible demonstration of "openness" allowed by the government at that time.

I went back to China a few years ago. The change and the progress in the human condition were profound. What had been gray now had a rainbow of color. Economic development—and the entrepreneurial spirit—was evident around every corner. The streets were still crowded, but this time jammed with cars. And the newspapers plastered on walls had been supplanted by cell phones and laptop computers with Internet access. There was an openness that I believed was virtually irreversible, although much progress still needs to be made.

Two personal stories: (a) when first in China, a colleague used a Polaroid camera and the Chinese people thought a miracle had been wrought. They had never before seen themselves in print. Today, Eastman Kodak sells more film in China than in any other country in the world outside the United States; (b) when last in China, a human rights activist said to me, "Let's keep in touch. What's your e-mail address?" That's progress.

I have no doubt that commercial relations between China and the United States—and the rest of the world—contributed substantially to these changes in Chinese society. Mao's approach was wrong, and the actions, if not the words, of subsequent leaders in Beijing have demonstrated that they know he was wrong. They have opted for a movement toward a market economy, with all that means for progress and development and, ultimately and inevitably, various forms of freedom.

This view is also held by both President Jimmy Carter and President Bill Clinton, by both Vice President Al Gore and Senator Bill Bradley, by both Governor George W. Bush and Senator John McCain, by both Senators from New York and by both Senate candidates in New York.

I believe that bringing China further into the international economic system will only accelerate these trends. And I am persuaded that these trends enhance freedoms for the Chinese people which, in turn, should make Asia and the world more secure.

Bilateral U.S.–China Trade

Looking at this purely in commercial terms, it seems fairly clear that the consequences of rejection of PNTR on U.S. businesses generally would be quite severe. There is virtual unanimity in the busi-

---

Welcoming China into the WTO . . . and stabilizing our trading relations with that massive and growing market is in our economic interest.

---

ness community that welcoming China into the WTO—which will happen regardless of how the upcoming vote in Congress goes—and stabilizing our trading relations with that massive and growing market is in our economic interest. And if that were the only criterion on which to base our vote, the decision would be easy indeed.

We should also keep in mind that the vote is solely on the status of our trading relationship with China. It is *not* a vote on whether to permit China to join the WTO. That will happen regardless of how Congress votes. The agreement before us contains provisions which substantially open up China's market to U.S. goods and services, but it does not open our market wider to China's exports. If we approve the agreement, our business community will be able to compete on a level field with European, Japanese and other exporters seeking to expand their business in China. But if we disapprove it, firms from elsewhere in the world will have a major leg up on American exporters, threatening our ability to participate in the growth of the Chinese market and reducing the number of American jobs that would otherwise be created as our trade with China builds.

Even if we wanted to, we cannot build an economic wall around China and one-fifth of the world's people. Outsiders will trade with China; the only question is whether and to what extent they will be Americans. I fear that opposing this agreement would be tantamount to building a wall around ourselves, trying to deal with the world by ignoring it. Throughout the 20th century we have seen all too often how ineffective such an approach can be.

These points were among those made just last week by Federal Reserve Board Chairman Alan Greenspan when he went to the White House to endorse approval of normalizing trade relations with China.

Looked at from the perspective of New York State, and from my role as the ranking Democrat on the Banking Committee, the case is equally strong. New York's financial services industry is a key source of economic growth and job creation—in the state and nationally—and this agreement will be of enormous economic benefit to that industry.

This is not to say that the business community has been entirely right in its approach to this issue. Quite the contrary. American business leaders have almost refused to acknowledge that the concerns about workers' rights, human rights, religious freedom and the environment are legitimate ones. They have resisted calls for even minimal standards in these areas. What they fail to recognize is that trade requires both capital and labor, and that therefore it's not inappropriate for a trade deal to address concerns of both capital and labor. What they ignore in this situation, as they have so often here at home, is that environmental degradation is a real cost of doing business, just one that doesn't happen to show up on their balance sheet. I wish that there had been greater recognition of these legitimate concerns by the business community as this debate progressed.

Jobs and Workers' Rights

My friends in the labor movement express concerns that approving the China agreement might mean loss of jobs in the U.S. And they also express concerns that a vote for the agreement might be seen as approval of some of the very serious ways in which the regime in China undermines workers' rights there.

These are real concerns. I do not make light of them. The labor leaders who express them are not alarmists; they are in the great tradition of leaders who have helped make the United States the most productive economy in the world; leaders who played such a large role in bringing down communism in the former Soviet Union and eastern Europe.

But I also have deep respect for other labor leaders who take a different view. One is both the former President of the U.A.W. and the former Ambassador to China, Leonard Woodcock. No one would ever describe him as naive, and he was one of the most forceful and effective leaders the United Auto Workers ever had. His view of the proposed trade agreement is that it is an imperative to advance our national interests.

Human Rights and Religious Freedom

The leadership in Beijing, while improving the human condition of the Chinese people in many ways over the past twenty years, still has demonstrated inadequate concern. I abhor, for example, population policies which condone and sometimes even demand forced abortions. Freedom of speech and association, among our most cher-

---

If the Chinese see and interact with Americans, tourists and business men and women, they will see what freedom brings and will demand, and get, more freedoms for themselves.

---

ished treasures, are still being developed in China. And too often, individuals are discriminated against because of their religious beliefs.

In the 19th century, our nation was abhorred, and rightly so, because of slavery. And subsequently, well into the 20th century, our society condoned or tolerated lynchings, burnings, and massive racial discrimination including denial of the most fundamental right, the right to vote. Those policies are and were wrong, our nation was wrong. We were equally wrong in denying women the vote for so long. But, fortunately, we were not ostracized from the world community. Rather, other countries dealt with us, despite our shortcomings, and we with them, despite their failures. Our nation evolved and improved, without others seeking to impose their approaches on us. They engaged us, and we learned.

I believe that influencing human rights in another country can be done far more effectively through engagement than through isolation. I believe that if we immerse China with American people and products, it will generate broader freedoms in that nation. I believe that if the Chinese see and interact with Americans, tourists and business men and women, they will see what freedom brings and will demand, and get more freedoms for themselves.

We should not ignore the situation in Tibet or the recent efforts to suppress the Falun Gong. And some human and religious rights advocates, from China and elsewhere, think that disapproval of PNTR will enhance the cause of freedom inside China. But there are many other human and religious rights advocates who disagree strongly. For example, the views of Martin Lee and other human rights advocates in Hong Kong are particularly striking, to say nothing of the new democratic leaders in Taiwan, and the Dalai Lama. They believe that engagement with China and approval of PNTR will advance the cause of human rights in mainland China.

Moreover, individuals in the United States who have dedicated their lives to advancing human rights and religious freedom for the people of China support granting PNTR with China. President Jimmy Carter argues persuasively that a negative vote would deal a serious setback to further democratization, freedom and human rights in China. Prominent Catholics, among them former-Member of Congress, Father Robert F. Drinan; University of Notre Dame President-Emeritus Father Theodore Hesburgh; and Father Peter Ruggere with the Maryknoll Fathers all support PNTR for China and believe it is how the U.S. can best advance human rights and religious freedom for the people of China. And the Quakers have expressed their belief that normalization of trade with China will advance all of the basic human security concerns—human rights, labor rights, arms control, and environmental protection—to which they are dedicated.

As we rightly criticize China for policies that we abhor, let us also remember that she has done some things that are very praiseworthy as well. China is a poor nation, relatively speaking, but, if nothing else, they have found ways to ensure that their vast population has enough to eat. The poverty level in China is only nine percent, versus a poverty level of over 40% in India. Further, during the recent economic crisis in Asia, China stood the course, resisting the lure of steps which might have helped their economy in the short term (such as devaluation of their currency) but which would have meant much more serious problems for the entire region in the longer term. Finally, China has allowed and is supporting the spread of phones—from virtually none to about 130 million in a generation—and access to the Internet for millions—the greatest democratizing tool the world has ever known, for it brings ideas from every corner of the world. Clearly, the ability to communicate is a fundamental right that has grown dramatically because of our twenty years of engagement.

International Security and Geopolitics

China is arguably the second strongest conventional military power in the world, and of course it is also a member of the nuclear club, with a small but growing capability to deliver nuclear arms. China's relations with her neighbors—Russia and India in particular—become difficult at times. And the situation concerning Taiwan is potentially the hottest "hot spot" in Asia if not the world.

We should not approve PNTR simply because it might help ease tensions in Asia. But it is most appropriate to include this consideration in assessing PNTR. And in that light, it is illuminating to look within China and see how various segments of their society view the move toward broader trade relations with the U.S. and others.

The fact is that the hard-liners in the Chinese government and military oppose or are lukewarm, at best, about China joining the WTO and entering into the proposed agreement with the United States. They believe that taking these steps will enhance freedom inside China, and in so doing dilute their power and influence. I think they are right, and that this is one more reason to engage, rather than isolate. After all, the best way to defeat an enemy is not to best him on the field of battle, but to make him your friend. Disapproving PNTR will result in the hard-liners saying, "See, we told you so, America is hostile to us so we must guard against her." We should do what we can to bolster those in China who want to establish friendly relations with the rest of the world, rather than those who believe that might is the only thing that matters.

The Taiwan situation warrants our most careful attention. The war of words between Beijing and Taipei would lead one to think that there was little if any meaningful contact between Taiwan and the mainland. But that is not the case. Already the amount of trade between the robust economy on Taiwan and the mainland is huge, it is growing, and the economic links grow tighter and tighter. Taiwan's new leaders, proponents of freedom and capitalism, realize that their relations with the leaders in Beijing can enhance or threaten these economic ties. And they favor PNTR.

Avoiding Past Mistakes

As I have studied the situation with China, I have found myself reflecting more and more about mistakes made by the U.S. this century. Almost a century ago, we made a gigantic mistake in not joining the League of Nations, and it helped lead to war with Germany.

A half century ago, we made a gigantic mistake with regard to Cuba. I have concluded that our policies in that situation were seriously mistaken. I believe that if we had resisted imposing the embargo on Cuba, Castro would be history and democracy would be flourishing there as it is in almost every other nation of the western hemisphere. Our effort to isolate Cuba has contributed mightily to keeping its economy from growing. But obviously they did not succeed in bringing about political change. Quite the contrary.

By letting a tiny but vocal minority dictate our Cuba policy, we missed an opportunity to send our message of freedom to the oppressed people there. We have strengthened Castro, unwittingly, and put ourselves in a situation where we have very little real influence on a nation only 90 miles from our shores.

We must not make the same mistakes with a country of 1.3 billion people that we made with a country of 10 million people. China has over 20 percent of the world's population; she is important, even vital, to world peace and prosperity in the decades ahead.

> ### *China must become part of the world community . . . or we will live in a more dangerous world for decades or longer.*

Conclusion

This agreement includes the strongest anti-surge controls ever legislated. We created the Congressional-Executive Commission on China to oversee every aspect of human rights, including worker rights. We negotiated a provision blocking imports from slave or prison labor. We fought for the creation of a specific inventory of the rights Congress will examine annually on behalf of the Chinese people. This new way of keeping the spotlight on Beijing is crucial, in my view, as we seek to build on the progress of the past.

China must become part of the world community, one way or another, or we will live in a more dangerous world for decades or longer. I think everyone involved in this debate agrees on that central point. The real question is how we can best influence continued change in China. Whatever choice this Congress makes, China will become a member of the WTO and an ever more important player in the global economy. That will inevitably impact on U.S. labor and U.S. business in ways we cannot avoid—only try to shape.

Labels help to shape the debate, of course. We talk about this being a vote on *Permanent* Normal Trade Relations with China. But is "permanent" the right word in a world where little is permanent, where laws can change from year to year? I don't think so. To my mind, the better words to use as a label for this issue would be *Continuance* of the Normal Trade Relations that have existed for 20 years. After all, this year's vote would simply end what has before been an annual automatic sunset on normal trade relations. But it would hardly prohibit Congress from re-visiting the matter next year or at any time in the future and sunsetting it with an affirmative vote, rather than by automatic operation of law. So those who say this is fraught with danger because of its "permanency" are, in my judgment, incorrect.

As I have reviewed this situation, I have frequently thought about the young people of China. A generation ago, Chinese students traveled to Moscow and learned the Russian language and Marxist-Leninist doctrine. Now, the children of these students attend universities in New York City, Chicago, Los Angeles and Buffalo and Rochester.

The collaboration between the school of business at the University of Buffalo and its counterparts in two Chinese universities is a dramatic example. Graduates of those programs are now a successful and influential group of alumni inside China. I have no doubt that China benefits from this educational partnership. But I am also convinced that the United States benefits, too. American faculty and students learn about China while they learn about us. And the messages of capitalism and freedom are spread.

This is but a microcosm of what engagement can mean. Look at what happened in Poland. Americans found ways to interact with people in Poland. Our labor unions supplied Solidarity with computers and vast amounts of assistance and encouragement. No one can know exactly how significant these contacts were in bringing the communist regime down and setting the stage for dismemberment of the old Soviet empire. But what we do know is that they did play a part, and the world is a better place for it.

My vote, Mr. Speaker, is for engagement and against isolation. Our leadership in the world requires it.

Picking up the Pieces[3]

Clinton's Foreign Policy

Kim R. Holmes

Vice president and director, Kathryn and Shelby Cullom Davis Institute for International Studies, The Heritage Foundation, 1992– ; B.A. in history, University of Central Florida, 1974; M.A., 1977, and Ph.D., 1982, in history, Georgetown University; adjunct professor, Georgetown University, 1982; senior fellow, Institute for Foreign Policy Analysis; defense policy analyst, Heritage Foundation, 1985; director of Foreign and Defense Policy Studies and Senior Policy Analyst for national security affairs at Heritage Foundation, until 1992; member of Council on Foreign Relations and its Washington Advisory Committee; Executive Committee and Board of Directors, Center for International Private Enterprise; co-editor, Issues 2000: The Candidate's Briefing Book; Restoring American Leadership: A U.S. Foreign and Defense Policy Blueprint; Index of Economic Freedom; *and* Mandate for Leadership IV and Defending America: A Near-and-Long Term Plan to Deploy Missile Defenses.

Editors' introduction: Kim R. Holmes suggested to 1,000 delegates attending the annual Conservative Political Action Conference (CPAC) that, "while our military commitments to places like Bosnia and Kosovo have grown in number, our military forces have steadily become smaller and weaker." According to Dr. Holmes, President Clinton's "poor performance" in foreign policy decisions was caused by three factors: politics, ideology, and neglect.

Kim Holmes' speech: I would like to start by asking all of you to think back to the 1980 presidential election. Remember when Ronald Reagan asked the American people "are you better off today than you were four years ago?"

I would like to put a similar question to President Clinton. My question is this: "Is the world better off today than it was eight years ago when Bill Clinton took office?" And related to that, "is America more secure today than it was eight years ago?"

3. Delivered to Conservative Political Action Conference (CPAC) 2000 Conference, Arlington, Virginia, January 21, 2000, 2:30 p.m.. Reprinted with permission of Kim R. Holmes.

Let's look at the record. Eight years ago Russia was awash in hope and promise. Boris Yeltsin was pro-American. He offered cooperation on a whole host of issues—even missile defense and European security. Yeltsin was a democratic hero, and his democratic allies were the dominant political force in Russia.

Today, after eight years of Clinton's leadership, Yeltsin is gone, replaced by a former KGB man who has allied himself with the communists. The democrats of yesteryear are playing very little role in Russian politics. Corruption is rampant (and possibly even behind the transfer of power from Yeltsin to Putin), Russia is engaged in its second brutal war in Chechnya, and Russian foreign policy is routinely hostile to and resentful of the United States.

Or look at Iraq. Eight years ago Saddam Hussein was locked in a tightly closed box. Iraq was defeated and isolated. He faced strong internal opposition, especially in the Kurdish areas of Iraq. There was an international consensus that only an effective and highly intrusive inspection regime could keep Iraq from getting nuclear weapons. Even the United Nations backed U.S. policy to contain Saddam Hussein.

Today, Saddam has broken out of that box. Clinton allowed Saddam to crush the Kurdish opposition to his regime in 1996. The international inspection regime to stop Saddam from acquiring nuclear weapons is shattered. The international consensus so painstakingly assembled by George Bush to contain Saddam Hussein exists no more. Today we have no idea what Saddam is doing with his weapon programs.

Or let's look at the Balkans, a place where the administration claims a great success. In 1992 there was a terrible war raging in the Balkans, but it was confined mainly to Bosnia. Conservatives at the time wanted to lift the arms embargo on the Bosnian Muslims and supply them with arms, partly to avoid the need to get the United States directly involved in Balkan politics and security. Shortly after he took office, President Clinton promised never to send U.S. forces to Bosnia.

Eight years later, of course, the Balkan war that was supposed to stop in Bosnia spread to Kosovo, and U.S. forces are now deployed not only in Bosnia but in Kosovo. This was practically inevitable once Clinton ruled out arming the Bosnian Muslims. What is worse, it became inevitable, too, because all of Clinton's Balkan deals ended up propping up Serbian strongman, Slobodon Milosovic, who now is threatening his next victim, Montenegro.

Such has been the sad story of Clinton's Balkan policy: America's military involvement grows, while the root of the problem—Milosovic—still survives to cause trouble another day.

Our military involvement in Bosnia and Kosovo points to another problem facing American security: all the while our military commitments to places like Bosnia and Kosovo have grown in number, our military forces have steadily become smaller and weaker.

Again, let's look at the record. Eight years ago, on the heels of a great military victory in the gulf war, our armed forces were the mightiest military machine the world had ever seen. Military readiness and morale were at a peak. Retention rates were high. We were meeting or exceeding our recruiting goals.

Today, our armed forces are a shadow of their former greatness. The Pentagon admits that many of our units are not ready for combat. The morale of our forces are so low that it is proving

> *Today, our armed forces are a shadow of their former greatness.*

impossible to retain good people and to attract new ones. Military pay is so low that some of our troops are on food stamps. Defense spending is down 15% and the size of our forces have shrunk by one fourth from the time when Clinton first took office.

Ladies and gentlemen, President Clinton squandered our military strength like a spoiled rich kid running through his father's inheritance.

The president squandered a tremendous lead as well in the area of missile defense—our effort to build a capability to defend this nation from the growing threat of ballistic missile attack.

Eight years ago, Bill Clinton inherited a robust program that would have begun deployment of global missile defense capability by 1997. I repeat by 1997—three years ago. Great progress had been made in the research and development of an entire family of advanced technologies—ground, sea and space-based interceptors, advanced sensor technologies, and sophisticated command and control capabilities. We were even talking to the Russians about gaining their cooperation in building this global protection system.

But today, we are falling behind in the race to defend ourselves against a growing missile threat. President Clinton repeatedly delayed the decision to begin the deployment of missile defenses. The people around him are calling yet again for another delay beyond June of this year—the deadline for a deployment decision. Clinton terminated Reagan and Bush missile defense programs, cut in half the funding for missile defense development, killed the promising "brilliant pebbles" space-based interceptor program, and even walked out of talks with Russia on how to cooperate on curbing the threat to both of our countries.

And what has been the result? Lost time. Those who would threaten us with their missiles have stolen the march on us. All the while we cut back on our promising programs and technologies, the missile threat to this country grew. We now are facing the prospect that within a few years the craziest regime on earth—North Korea—could have a ballistic missile capable of incinerating cities in Alaska or California.

The Clinton administration has repeatedly claimed that curbing the proliferation of nuclear weapons and missiles was one of its highest priorities. But proliferation only became worse since Clinton took office. There were the nuclear tests in India and Pakistan, and the accelerated missile developments in North Korea, Iran and other rogue states. And need I remind this audience that the president's administration itself, through lax security measures, stands accused of enhancing the capabilities of China's nuclear programs.

I could go on. There are other examples of missed opportunities, broken promises, and outright mistakes. But these examples I give you today speak for themselves. Bill Clinton is not responsible for everything that has gone wrong in the world since he took office. But he is responsible enough—particularly since all he had to do was preserve the strong hand dealt to him by Bush and Reagan in 1992. And particularly since he has repeatedly told us that he wants to be remembered for his foreign policy accomplishments.

How do we account for Clinton's poor performance? Why did it happen that so many things that were so promising in the early part of the 1990s turned out so poorly at the start of the new millennium?

I see three reasons. The first involves politics. President Clinton never took foreign policy seriously. He tended to treat it like any other political issue with a particular constituency to please. The interventions in Haiti and Somalia were done largely to please political allies in Congress and elsewhere. The timing for the interventions in Bosnia in 1995 was mainly political, intending to neutralize Bob Dole in the 1996 presidential election. The flip-flop on China before the last election was driven largely by fund-raising concerns, to curry favor with the business community. And the recent flip-flop on trade at the Seattle summit was all about politics—to please the unions and environmentalists and to help get Al Gore elected president.

Ladies and gentlemen, I will not contend that other presidents have not been guilty of playing politics with foreign policy. But Clinton raised this practice to a new level. What is different with Clinton is that politics was the main driving force, the essential reason for the action, not a secondary factor that shaped public relations or shaded how it was implemented.

Another reason for this poor performance involves ideology. Notwithstanding his claim of being a New Democrat, the president is steeped in what I call post-cold war liberalism. This is a new species of liberalism. Its roots are in the old Cold War, but it has adapted to a new environment. The best examples of this new species are so-called humanitarian operations—of the kind we have seen in Somalia, Haiti, Bosnia and Kosovo. Under Clinton these kinds of operations have exploded, much to the detriment of our military readiness, and to our sense of priorities.

Another example is environmental globalism, as reflected in the Kyoto protocol, an international treaty which Clinton signed to ban the emission of carbon gases into the atmosphere. The goal here is to get around Congress—to do through international treaties and organizations what cannot be accomplished by the domestic political process: namely, to regulate the American economy.

> *The world is a more dangerous place today than it was in 1992. And America is less secure.*

The third cause was neglect. President Clinton never really warmed up to foreign policy. It had too little political benefit to engage his mind in any systematic way. He paid attention to foreign policy issues only episodically, and mainly when media attention or political benefits were promised, or when crises forced themselves upon him.

Thus important and difficult issues were ignored. Things drifted. Problems became worse. Despite promises to the contrary, the president neglected our defenses, allowing them to become perilously weak. Despite numerous summits, he let our policy toward Russia drift and became little more than an echo of the International Monetary Fund. He ignored Bosnia until the 1996 election loomed on the horizon; he then, in a political panic, ordered his staff to do something quickly to get the story off the front pages of the newspapers.

As a result, the world is a more dangerous place today than it was in 1992. And America is less secure.

So what do we do now? How can we pick up the pieces? We need a president who takes foreign policy seriously. Foreign policy and national security are not political playthings. Nor should they be an excuse to bathe in the eye of the media and world opinion. They are very serious business. As John F. Kennedy used to say, "domestic policy can only defeat us; foreign policy can kill us." We need a president who understands not only the seriousness of the task at hand, but of the opportunities. We are the most powerful nation on earth, and we can shape our destiny and the destiny of the world like no other country in human history. This is not a task for small-minded leaders who obsess on opinion polls and treat foreign policy as a form of constituency politics or as a photo-opportunity.

We need to get past this post–cold war liberal ideological mind-set I described earlier—the one that says that real wars are over for America, and probably should not be fought anyway, and that the only proper use of American power is for peacekeeping and humanitarian causes.

Ladies and gentlemen, if we continue down this path, our military forces will be over-committed, our enemies will be legion, and our foreign policy morally confused—even hypocritical. We will never be unable to explain why we fight in Kosovo but not in Rwanda, Burundi, the Ivory Coast or some other strategically unimportant place embroiled in terrible conflict. This path leads to a dead end. It will be only a matter of time until we see another Somalia or even Vietnam—where an enemy, who cares more about its cause than we do about ours, exacts a price higher than we are willing to pay. So far, except for Somalia, we have been lucky. This luck will not last forever.

And finally, we need to get back to basics in foreign policy. We need to focus mainly on what only we can do, and what we do best. That is mainly two things: 1) maintain through military strength a global balance of power in favor of our security and interests, and in favor of the forces of freedom and democracy; 2) maintain our economic leadership in the world and our commitment to free and open markets. Everything else is secondary. To accomplish these goals, we need to restore our military strength; deploy a missile protection system as quickly as possible; reshape our military alliances so our allies share a bigger burden of defense; regain our leadership role in international trade; and focus like a laser on big ticket priority items, like China and Russia. Thank you.

The Jesuit Martyrs of El Salvador[4]

James P. McGovern

Representative from Massachusetts (D), U.S. House of Representatives, 1997– ; born, Worcester, MA, November 20, 1959; B.A., 1981, and Masters of Public Administration, 1984, American University; managed Senator George McGovern's 1984 presidential campaign in Massachusetts; gave McGovern's nomination speech, 1984 Democratic National Convention, San Francisco; selected by U.S. Representative John Joseph Moakley to lead a Congressional investigation into the murders of six Jesuit priests and two lay women in El Salvador, 1989; Regional Whip, House Democratic Leadership team; member, House Transportation and Infrastructure Committee, 1997– ; serves on Subcommittee on Aviation and Subcommittee on Water Resources and Environment; Jesuit International Volunteers Board of Directors.

Editors' introduction: Representative James P. McGovern spoke at the Jesuit-run University of Central America (UCA) at the invitation of the Association of Jesuit Colleges and Universities to commemorate the 10th anniversary of the murders of the UCA's Jesuit leadership. He addressed an audience of more than 400, including faculty, students, dignitaries, and religious representatives from across El Salvador and elsewhere. Also present were family members of the six Jesuit priests and two lay women who were murdered in 1989 on the UCA campus. In the speech below, Mr. McGovern, while believing "with all my heart that the United States is a great country," concluded that "the actions of my government . . . during the long years of the Salvadoran war, were a source of deep disappointment." The speech, which was favorably received, was carried live over the radio stations of the university and the Salvadoran Catholic Church. It was also reprinted in *Proceso*, the UCA monthly newsletter, and other Catholic publications.

James P. McGovern's speech: I feel privileged to be here tonight, to be part of this company of speakers, to hear the words and memories of the families, and to honor and remember the lives of our friends—Ignacio Ellacuria, Segundo Montes, Ignacio, Martin-Baro, Amando Lopez, Juan Ramon Moreno, Joaquin Lopez y Lopez, Elba Julia Ramos and Celina Ramos. Congressman Moakley and I are most associated with the investigation into their murders, but I was honored to know these priests for many years. I was

4.   Delivered in San Salvador, El Salvador, on November 12, 1999, 7:30 p.m. Reprinted with permission of James P. McGovern.

honored to call them my friends. I learned from their insights, research and analysis. I laughed and sang songs with them. And I have been inspired by the lives they led.

The lives and deaths of my friends and my experiences in El Salvador have informed and influenced all other actions I have taken on human rights issues. They shape the way I tackle the challenges of social justice, fairness, and civil rights in my own country. And they are always in my thoughts as I think about the values and ideals I wish to pass along to my 18-month-old son, Patrick George McGovern.

The actions of my government, . . . during the long years of the Salvadoran war, were a source of deep disappointment for me because U.S. policy did not reflect the values and ideals of America.

I believe with all my heart that the United States is a great country. That it is built upon the promotion and preservation of freedom, liberty and respect for the rights and dignity of every one of our citizens. The U.S. has fought to protect democracy, helped war-ravaged countries rebuild, and responded generously to natural disasters, like Hurricane Mitch. As someone who values a sense of history, I'm inspired by the principles enshrined in our founding documents.

The actions of my government, however, during the long years of the Salvadoran war, were a source of deep disappointment for me because U.S. policy did not reflect the values and ideals of America. Instead, that policy had more to do with our obsession with the Cold war than with the search for peace and justice in El Salvador.

The U.S. did not cause the war in El Salvador. But our policy did help prolong a war that cost tens of thousands of innocent lives—including the lives of the six men and two women were gather to honor tonight. Had we used our influence earlier to promote a negotiated settlement, perhaps our friends might be here celebrating with us.

We in the United States need to acknowledge that fact. In particular, our leaders need to acknowledge that fact.

There was an arrogance about U.S. policy that rationalized, explained away, and even condoned a level of violence against the Salvadoran people that would have been intolerable if perpetrated against our own citizens.

Presidents, Vice Presidents, Senators and Members of Congress have for years come to El Salvador to tell you what changes you must make in your nation. They—and I—have urged you to make institutional changes in El Salvador—in your military, your police, your judiciary, and your political institutions. And you have made changes, and you have made great progress in these areas.

To be frank, however, they and I have rarely talked about the institutional changes we need to make in the United States. But the fact is, we in the U.S. have a responsibility to change the culture and mind-set of many of our own institutions.

I fear that we in the U.S. have institutions—namely our military and intelligence agencies—that have not fully learned the lessons of El Salvador. While there are examples where these agencies

---

> *Our military institutions should care as much about the lives and security of ordinary citizens as they do about strategic advantage and military relations.*

---

have performed admirably, we continue to make many of the same mistakes. Sadly, the U.S. continues to train, equip and aid repressive militaries around the world in the name of strategic interest— no matter the level of human rights abuses.

In late August, I traveled to East Timor. I was there nine days before the historic vote for independence. I spent a day out in the countryside with Catholic priests Hilario Madeira and Francisco Soares, who were protecting over 2,000 displaced people who had sought refuge from militia violence in the church courtyard. I had dinner in the home of Bishop Carlos Belo and heard him talk about the escalating violence against East Timorese people. And I thought about El Salvador, and the pastoral work of the Catholic Church, and my friends, the Jesuits, and the work of the UCA.

Two weeks after I returned to the United States, Father Hilario and Father Francisco were murdered, shot down on the steps of their church as they tried to protect their parishioners from massacre. Bishop Belo's house was burned to the ground, and he was forced to flee his country.

During the 24 years of Indonesian occupation of East Timor, the United States sent the Indonesian military over $1 billion in arms sales and over $500 million in direct aid and training. To the credit of the Clinton Administration, the U.S. severed military relations with Indonesia in September. But we should have done that sooner, and it was the Pentagon that was most reluctant to break relations with its military partners during the first critical weeks of violence that devastated the people of East Timor.

The problem with the Indonesian military, like the Salvadoran military of the 1980s, is not a problem of a "few bad apples." It is an institutional problem. And the U.S. approach to military aid, training and arms sales reflects an institutional problem within the U.S. military. *Never again should the United States be in the position of training and equipping military personnel who cannot distinguish between civilian actors and armed combatants.*

The U.S. has yet to sign the international treaty to ban antipersonnel land mines—a treaty the Government of El Salvador to its great credit has signed. You have seen the devastation of land mines—the tragedy of a young child missing a leg or an arm and maybe even missing a future. But why hasn't the U.S. yet signed the treaty? Because the institutional culture of the Pentagon rejects giving up any kind of weapon currently in its arsenal, no matter how deadly to innocent civilians. This must change.

Our military institutions *should* care as much about the lives and security of ordinary citizens as they do about strategic advantage and military relations. I have met many good men and women who serve in the Armed Forces, including many who serve in El Salvador. It is important that our institutions, like these individuals, realize that respecting human rights and safeguarding the lives of ordinary people *is* in the strategic and national interests of the United States.

And let me be clear, the U.S. Congress also must fulfill its responsibility and demand accountability of our military programs. All too often, Members of Congress simply don't want to know what our military and other programs abroad are doing.

We also must change the culture of secrecy and denial within our military and intelligence institutions.

I have pushed my government hard to disclose all documents in its possession related to the case of the four U.S. churchwomen murdered in El Salvador in 1980. It's been 19 years—and the families of these murdered women still do not have the satisfaction of knowing all that their government knows.

I have also pushed my government to release all documents relating to the Pinochet case, including materials on the United States role in the overthrow of the government of Chile and its aftermath. The people of Chile have waited 26 years for justice. The action taken by Spanish Judge Garzon has broken new ground in international human rights law, making it clear that no one, no matter how high their office, who commits crimes against humanity, can escape the consequences of their actions.

I don't do this because I can't let go of the past. I do this because I want to ensure a better future. It is hard to change "old ways"—whether we are talking about institutions in the United States or in El Salvador. But we must change in order to protect the freedoms of tomorrow.

I believe the United States has a special obligation, given our past, to help El Salvador in its economic development, to assist the people of El Salvador in achieving their goals, and to support the rights of Salvadoran refugees still living in the United States. As a Member of the U.S. Congress, I believe it is *my responsibility* to fight for more resources to aid in the development of El Salvador; to help El Salvador confront the challenges of poverty and inequality that limit the futures of so many Salvadoran families; and to aid the people of this great country in pursuing their dreams and aspirations.

I'm proud of our current programs in El Salvador. I know our Ambassador and U.S. AID director have made it a priority to reach out to the Salvadoran people, to encourage participation in the planning of United States development projects, and to forge a working relationship with communities throughout El Salvador—and I commend them for their fine work.

As a citizen of the United States, I want my country to be, in the words of my good friend and mentor, George McGovern, "a witness to the world for what is just and noble in human affairs." This will require the citizens of my country to bring our nation to a higher standard—and we will do so with respect and a deep love for our country.

Over a decade ago, the Jesuits of the UCA taught me that a life committed to social justice, to protecting human rights, to seeking the truth is a life filled with meaning and purpose. I hope my life will be such a life. And if it is, it will be due to my long association with the Jesuits, the UCA, and the people of El Salvador. And for that, I thank you—all of you—you who are here tonight, and those who are with us every day in spirit. You are truly "presente" in my life.

Cumulative Speaker Index: 1990–2000

A cumulative speaker index to the volumes of *Representative American Speeches* for the years 1937–1938 through 1959–1960 appears in the 1959–1960 volume; for the years 1960–1961 through 1969–1970, see the 1969–1970 volume; for the years 1970–1971 through 1979–1980, see the 1979–1980 volume; and for the years 1980–1981 through 1989–1990, see the 1989–1990 volume.

Index

207